AF073264

WHAT THE 'BOYS' DID OVER THERE

WHAT THE 'BOYS' DID OVER THERE
BY 'THEMSELVES'

EDITED BY
Henry L. Fox

This edition published in 2021 by Arcturus Publishing Limited
26/27 Bickels Yard, 151–153 Bermondsey Street,
London SE1 3HA

Copyright © Arcturus Holdings Limited

All rights reserved. No part of this publication may be reproduced, stored in a retrieval system, or transmitted, in any form or by any means, electronic, mechanical, photocopying, recording or otherwise, without prior written permission in accordance with the provisions of the Copyright Act 1956 (as amended). Any person or persons who do any unauthorised act in relation to this publication may be liable to criminal prosecution and civil claims for damages.

AD010128US

Printed in the UK

CONTENTS

IN MEMORIAM 7
INTRODUCTION 9
MY EXPERIENCE AS A DISPATCHER 13
BRINGING IN A "SNIPER" 21
ON THE FLANDERS FRONT 27
A "DEVIL DOG'S" STORY 31
IN THE VERDUN SECTOR 37
THE HUN I WAS SURE I "GOT" 41
LIFE IN THE TRENCHES 43
TWO YEARS IN THE YPRES SALIENT 47
A NIGHT ADVENTURE 53
A MACHINE GUNNER'S STORY 55
THE FALL OF CANTIGNY 61
THE RETREAT FROM MONS 67
MY SERVICE IN FLANDERS 73
MY SERVICE IN FLANDERS (PART TWO) 77
WITH THE AMMUNITION TRAIN 81
HOSPITAL EXPERIENCE 85
TWO YEARS AND A HALF OF WAR 89
FROM ENGLAND TO FRANCE AND BACK 95
"WHY I HATE A GERMAN" 103
"MY DUTY TO MY COUNTRY" 109
THE "DARDANELLES" CAMPAIGN 115
"THE FIRST OF THE TANKS" 121
THE SUNSHINE OF THE TRENCHES 125
MY EXPERIENCES IN FRANCE WITH THE 10th
    CANADIAN INFANTRY 133
THREE YEARS AND TWO MONTHS IN FRANCE 143

In Memoriam

This book is affectionately dedicated to "The Boys" who found their final rest in the Hallowed Soil of Martyred Belgium and France, by their more fortunate comrades.

THE AUTHORS

INTRODUCTION

How and Why This Book Was Compiled

By the Editor

IN ASSEMBLING the stories contained in this book we have endeavored to put in realistic and readable form some of the actual, and authentic, experiences of soldiers and officers of the Allied Forces, who have returned to their homes after nobly sacrificing themselves in the service of their respective countries. It has been our endeavor to give to these stories as much of the personality of "The Boys," who have told us their experiences, as possible, by using their own words whenever their physical condition permitted them to write their own stories.

Literary style has been a secondary consideration as we believe that a majority of the public would prefer to read the truth unabridged, than a story garbled by editorial tinkering.

We are indebted to the following heroes for their aid in the publication of this book:

Private Jesse W. Wade, Dispatch rider No. 151023. Wounded by shrapnel in the shoulder in Flanders, wounded in the leg at Soissons, Veteran of the Mexican campaigns of

1914 and 1916. Seven times cited for gallantry by the French Government.

Sergt. Jack Winston, No. 55525, 19th Batt., Canadian Infantry, 2nd Canadian Contingent. Wounded in the right arm, left ankle, and right knee. Shell-shocked and buried; also gassed at second battle of Ypres.

Pvt. Al. Barker, No. 118, 43rd Co., 5th Regt., American Marines. Shot in the knee and gassed at Chateau-Thierry, bayonet wounds in both feet at the Marne.

Corp. Frank J. Sears, Co. A, 9th Infantry, 2nd Div., A.E.F. Shell-shocked and gassed at Chateau-Thierry. Decorated by the French Government with the "Croix de Guerre."

Private A. F. Edwards, No. 6857, 1st Batt., 1st Brigade, 1st Div., Canadian Inf. Wounded in the right hand, right arm and buried by shell.

Machine gunner George Eckhart, No. 105688, First M. G. Batt., 1st Div., A.E.F. Wounded in the leg and gassed at Cantigny. Decorated by the French Government with the "Croix de Guerre."

Sergt. T. S. Grundy, 15918, Royal Fusileers, Middlesex Regt., English Army. Wounded in shoulder at Ypres and gassed at Loos. Decorated by the British Government with the "Mons Star." One of the first hundred thousand.

Sergt. Alexander Gibb, No. 444476, 26th Batt., New Brunswick Regt., 2nd Canadian Contingent. Wounded in both legs, shell-shocked, and gassed at Ypres.

F. G. McAvity, No. 91805, gunner of the 8th Battery, 1st Canadian Field Artillery. Wounded in the left foot, left thigh, left shoulder and gassed.

Sergt. Frederick Ralph Muir, No. 81611, 10th Batt., C.E.F. Wounded at Festubert, Belgium. Leg amputated at the knee.

Private George Oxton, 10th Batt., C.E.F., No. 81680. Wounded at Festubert, Belgium. Right leg amputated at hip.

Pvt. John Miller, No. 122957, 96th Co., 6th Regt., U. S. Marines.

Pvt. Jack Kneeland, No. 105, 43rd Co., 5th Regt., American Marines. Shrapnel wound in the head at Belleau Woods, wounded and gassed at Chateau-Thierry.

Sergt. Mark L. Nicholson, No. 3736, 10th Liverpool Scottish, B.E.F. Wounded in head at Dardanelles. Partially blinded and gassed, Hooge, France.

Sergt. E. D. G. Aylen, No. 475337, Princess Patricia's Canadian Light Infantry ("Princess Pats"). Blinded in right eye at Hooge, France. Wounded in left shoulder.

Sergt. Harry Hall, No. 19805, A Co., 10th Battalion, 1st Canadian Contingent. Shrapnel wounds, left arm and leg, Givenchy, June, 1915.

Lance Corporal Edmund Hall, 2nd Scottish Rifles, B.E.F. Regular Army, 15 years' service, 3½ in France. Wounded, Battle of Somme, 1916. Decoration, Star of Mons.

It is the hope of the authors that "What The Boys Did Over There" will give to its readers some idea of real conditions in the field, and bring to those of us who remained at home a realization of the debt we owe to the men who have suffered for us.

MY EXPERIENCE AS A DISPATCHER

*By Pvt. Jesse W. Wade,
No. 151023, Dispatch Rider, A.E.F.*

I ENLISTED in the U. S. Army some five years ago, and have had continuous service ever since. Being in the army before the war broke out enabled me to know something about both sides of army life, but peace times and war times are as different as day and night. One war is enough for any man, so now I am ready to settle down, but, before I do, I will endeavor to tell you some of my experiences in this Great War "Over Seas."

Being already in the army, but in a branch of the service that was not likely to go over among the first, I volunteered to go with the first contingent as a dispatcher. We started the first leg of our journey across the Atlantic, and then we began those anxious nights of watching for submarines—and that awful seasickness for some twelve days. At last we set our feet on solid ground again and started our long journey across France, in some French cattle cars marked eight horses or forty men. About three days in one of those, and one really believes there is a war going on somewhere. We were all very much disappointed when we were all landed a long way from the Front, and told we would stay there until we were trained in modern warfare; but all being blue-blooded Americans we took it very easy, building camps and getting things ready for the other boys that were coming.

The small village near our camps was full of our boys every night. Mumm's Extra Dry Champagne was selling at 2½ francs per quart (49c. U. S.). It wasn't very long before our boys were taking baths in champagne. After having a few weeks of camp life there were fifty men picked out, to go to the English front, to receive instructions in modern warfare. I was among the lucky ones, and then the *fun* of war began. We were sent to one of the most active British fronts, and there we lived in the trenches night and day for two months.

There I began to realize that Sherman's words were only too true. Anyone who never had the misfortune to be in Flanders, up around Ypres, at the time, will never know the hardships that the British, and a few Americans had to go through. We stood it wonderfully well, though. We could have enjoyed ourselves much more on Broadway. But the French say: "c'est la guerre" (it's war).

We had been in the trenches some three weeks before we had the opportunity of going "Over the Top." One's feelings the first time he goes "Over the Top" can never be known to anyone but himself. One will be dozing on the firing step, and the platoon leader comes around and whispers in your ear to get ready. The time is set for 1.13 A.M. You can hardly talk above a whisper for the least noise draws fire from the enemy. As the time draws near, you look at your watch and see that you have only seven or eight minutes. Yet, you almost sink down and it seems as though the bones have gone out of your legs and back. The time is getting short, and at last the big guns open up, and something just seems to push you up and over. Before you are aware of what is happening you are out on No Man's Land, acting like a veteran. After one or two of these successful raids you do not think war is so bad after all. It is real fun, but you have not seen enough of it yet. Tommie says: "Wait till you have three years of it and you'll be bloody well sick of it, Sammy." One year was enough to make me sick of it. Another very pleasant job is to crawl out on No Man's Land some dark night on patrol, dragging yourself along on the ground, an inch at a time, for fear of being heard and fired upon, and just as you think everything is going fine you run over a twig and break it. It snaps and sounds like a ton of dynamite going up, and then they send up a star-shell to light up No Man's Land, and you begin to say your prayers.

Then all is quiet again and you finish your work and feel your way back to the trench. There is never a happier moment than when you drop back in your own trench, safe and sound, among friends. It was on one of the patrols that I got my first wounds. I was sent out about 1.30 A.M. with a patrol of English to do some very ticklish work, and, in cutting our way through some wire entanglements, the wire snapped and made a ringing noise and the Germans opened up on us, throwing everything at us but their shoes. We were giving them a receipt for all they sent us until, all at once, I began to feel sick and my arm became numb. I almost collapsed, but I knew that that was no place to act like a girl and faint, so I began crawling back toward our trench. It was hard to do, having only one hand free, but at last I crawled into the trench where I found another horror waiting. Our trench was full of gas and I did not have my gas mask on and as I got one breath of it I was finished, and the next thing I knew I was back in a nice little bed, between two white sheets, with a little blonde nurse smiling down at me. I thought that I had died and that I was in heaven until I heard a Tommy say:

"Where in Hell is me 'Fags,'" and then I knew I was not in heaven, but was not sure I was alive yet. At last I found out I was, for, about thirty minutes later, the gas began to make me sick. Gas sickness is the worst sickness in the world.

After three weeks in bed I was getting along fine and was sent to a convalescent hospital. There we had the time of our lives for two weeks, when we were sent back to duty. It was just like a homecoming to get back with our own boys again after everyone thought you were dead. Everything ran along smoothly for awhile until I was detailed as a dispatch rider, one of the most dangerous jobs in the army.

The average term of a dispatcher's life is just twenty-three minutes, so you can't blame me for taking out $10,000 worth of life insurance. At first it was not so dangerous, for our troops had not yet taken over any part of the line, but we had to make trips to the Front every day or two. At last we were ordered into the line and took over a sector of our own, and a prouder bunch of boys was not to be found. We were then doing what we had come over to do. Everything was quiet for the first few months, except for an occasional raiding party. We spent the hardest winter I ever put in, or ever want to, and if it had not been for the "cooties" we should have frozen, but they kept us scratching and moving and kept our blood in circulation. At last spring came and things became more active as we were getting more men on the Front. On the 18th day of July, 1918, it was just like turning out a bunch of hungry lions, for they turned us loose, and said "go get them." We have been "getting them" ever since. At Chateau-Thierry we began driving them back so fast that they threw the Prussians and Bavarians at us; all big fellows six foot and over, and very wicked fighters. Being a dispatch rider I was around some point of the line most all the time, and had the opportunity to go "Over the Top" with the boys when not otherwise occupied. Once in awhile the dispatch riders would be given twenty-four or forty-eight hours off during which we could do as we pleased. Most of us went up in the line, and "Over the Top" with the boys, or those who had any qualifications as a shot would go out with a sniping squad which was very interesting as well as dangerous. At one time I had the pleasure of going up in an observation balloon, and seeing the fighting from the German side. I have seen with my own eyes German officers driving their men into battle with a whip or the point of a gun. I have also seen some of the atrocities committed by the Hun in Belgium and along the borders of France. It just makes one's blood run cold to think of it, as some of you do. You ask why a boy wants to stand up and be shot down by those dogs? I'll tell you why. It is because he doesn't want his own mother, or sister, to be treated as the Belgians and French women and girls have been treated. Every man, woman, and child owes the deepest respect to any boy who has done his bit in the World War.

Now to get back to the Battle of Chateau-Thierry, and tell you a few of my own experiences. In that battle one of the most thrilling experiences happened to me. The fight began at 3.30 A.M., July 26. I had just ridden up to a section of our line where the enemy had started a box-barrage, which it is almost impossible to get through alive and is almost like madness to attempt. At this time it was important that a certain message be delivered at the rear. Such a message is sent with from two to six riders, so that one of them will be sure to get through. There were five of us there at the time, but, owing to the fact that I had just come back from a trip, the message was sent by the other four riders. We watched them, but not one of them got through the barrage. Then the commander looked at me, and I looked at him. He didn't say anything but his look had words in it, written in big letters, saying:

"It's up to you."

I'll admit that I was scared. Not the cowardly kind but a different kind of fear. I once heard a general say that a soldier's life was made up of four parts—"Smiles and tears, profanity and prayers," and I think I executed all four of them at the same instant. It was only a delay of a few moments as he had the fifth message already written out, and in his hand, so I jumped on my machine, grabbed the message, and was gone before he knew what it was all about. I delivered the message without a scratch, but I think I was insane at the time; for it all seems like a dream. It was nothing short of a miracle. The fighting was very heavy for some days after that, and there was a similar case that occurred shortly afterward. This time I was the only rider at hand and I had to go. But rather than take another chance with the barrage I could go across a corner of No Man's Land and circle around to the left. This avoided the barrage, but I had to face the enemy machine gun fire, which was very heavy. I started out on my last trip, as a dispatcher, and was not seen until going over a slight rise, when the enemy saw me. They opened up on me and threw everything at me but Iron Crosses. The machine gun was the worst, but after three minutes of hard riding, over rough ground, shell-holes, and craters, I was out of range of the machine guns. Then they began throwing the larger guns at me. My machine was riddled with bullets. The engine was about out of commission, but as I was through the worst of it and was shaking hands with myself on how lucky I had been, I realized that I had been hit in the leg and after the excitement had died down I was so weak I could not sit on my machine again. Good luck came along in the shape of a Frenchman and he helped me to headquarters some 500 yards away. I delivered the message and then collapsed and a few days later awoke in a French hospital in Paris. Since then I have been having the time of my life, and am back in the dear old U. S. now, almost well but willing to go through it all again for the same cause.

BRINGING IN A "SNIPER"

An Incident of the Battle of Kemmel Hill, Told by Sergt. "Jack" Winston, 55525, 19th Battalion, Canadian Infantry, 2nd Canadian Contingent.

ABOUT two hours before dawn on the morning of Oct. 8, 1915, my company were in a sector of the front line trenches near Kemmel Hill. My comrades were taking their ease, as we had been in comparative quiet for the previous three days. They were variously employed: some writing home, others idly smoking, the signal man lounging in the dugout near his telephone instrument, and sundry others doing their bit toward cleanliness by removing "cooties" from their shirts. Our lieutenant was looking hard across No Man's Land through the trench periscope, and I wondered what was keeping him so long looking at a spot I thought we all knew by heart. He stood there perfectly immovable for at least fifteen minutes, while several star-shells, fired both from our own lines and the German trenches, flared and died. Finally he turned to me and whispered, "Jack, I do not remember that dead horse out there yesterday. Take a look and tell me if you remember seeing it before." I looked at the spot indicated and sure enough there was a dead horse lying at the side of a shell-hole where I could have sworn there was nothing the day before.

I told the lieutenant I was sure that nothing had been there on the previous day, and waited for further orders. German snipers had annoyed us considerably and as they took great pains in concealing their nests we had little success in stopping them. Several casualties had resulted from their activities. The lieutenant had evidently been thinking, while taking his long observation, for he said almost at once: "I believe that nag is a neat bit of camouflage. One of those Huns is probably hidden in that carcass to get a better shot at us."

He then told me to have the men at the portholes fire at the carcass, at five second intervals, to keep "Fritz," if he were there, under cover—and taking advantage of the dark interval between the glare of the star-shells, he slipped "Over the Top," having told me he was going to get that Hun.

Imagine my suspense for the next half hour. I kept looking through the periscope but for fully fifteen minutes I could not find my officer. Finally I spotted him sprawled out, apparently dead, as a star-shell lit up the ground within the range of the periscope. As no shot had been fired, except from our portholes, I knew he was not as dead as he seemed. And sure enough when next I could make him out he was several yards ahead, and to the left, of the spot where I had last seen him. Then I knew what he was after. He was making a detour to approach the carcass from the rear, and as he could only move in the dark intervals between star-shells his progress was, of necessity, slow. At the end of another fifteen minutes I located him in a position, as nearly as I could judge, about ten yards in the rear and just a step to the left of the carcass. I then thought it time for me to take a hand, and give him what help I could.

Running into the signal man's dugout I told him to call for a barrage, giving the range at, approximately, thirty yards behind the point at which the carcass lay.

I then jumped back to the periscope only to see, by the next flare, that the lieutenant was no longer in sight. Leaving the periscope I selected three men, whom I was sure I could trust, and, by the time I had brought them to the firing step, the barrage from the guns in our rear for which the signal man had telegraphed began to fall.

Quickly explaining to the men what I had in mind, that we were going to help the lieutenant, I was about to give the order to go "Over the Top," when another man, who had overheard, begged me for permission to accompany us, and as I had need for someone to repair the barbed wire, which the lieutenant had cut on his way out, I gave him the job together with permission to go with us.

After a few words of instruction to the corporal, who, during my absence, was left in command of our sector, we went silently "Over the Top" at the point where the lieutenant had preceded us.

The barrage had by this time aroused the curiosity of the enemy and they were replying with a brisk shelling of our lines, and the batteries that were laying down the barrage.

We advanced at a walk and were fortunate enough to find the place where our lieutenant had cut his way through our barbed wire. There I left my volunteers with the necessary tools to repair the wire, after we should have passed through it on our return.

It was now beginning to get light enough for us to see several yards in either direction around us, and after moving forward about fifty yards beyond the wire, we ran straight into the lieutenant, who was driving the Hun before him at the muzzle of his automatic.

We wasted no time on the return journey but hustled "Fritzie" along at a brisk pace.

Just as we had passed back through the barbed wire, a piece of shrapnel struck my volunteer in the shoulder, and I was forced to stop, and leave a man to complete the repairs on the wire, while I helped the wounded man back to the trenches. The remaining men, who had started with me, had remained with the lieutenant and his prisoner, and we found all safe in the trench on our arrival.

My wounded man proved to be not seriously hurt and the man who remained to mend the wire also returned unhurt.

When all were safe in the trench, the lieutenant called off the barrage and the enemy in our front was doubtless wondering what it was all about, until the sniper, who, as the lieutenant surmised, was hidden in the camouflaged carcass, returned no more.

The lieutenant had arrived at a point about five paces behind the Hun before the sniper discovered him, and then had him covered with his automatic. Like most of his breed there was a wide "yellow streak" in this baby-killer and he cried "Kamerad" instantly. By the time the lieutenant had secured his prisoner's rifle our barrage was falling and, under its protection, he began his march back with the prisoner, and met us before he had gone twenty-five yards. The rest you know.

The prisoner expected to be killed at once and begged piteously for his life, saying "he had a wife and three children." One of the men replied that if he had his way he would make it a "widow and three orphans."

Needless to say he did not have his way, and for all I know that sniper is still eating three square meals per day in a prison camp.

ON THE FLANDERS FRONT

By Sergt. Jack Winston

IT WAS in November, 1915—we were at Kemmel Hill, when the wet weather started in. I remember one night I was sent out of the trenches to the Dump, near the dressing station, for rations. We had no communication trenches then, owing to the heavy shelling we were getting from the German artillery, and we never had the guns to come back at them. We had to go out at dusk through the fields, known to us as "overland." We got down to the dump all right, but coming back the Germans saw us, and they turned three machine guns on us. I was about fifty yards from the front line when the barrage started. My pal was just behind me. About four yards from us was an old French trench, with about three feet of water in it. I jumped into that with my pal. The Germans kept the barrage up for about a half an hour and as soon as it stopped I made my way for the front lines.

Just imagine what condition I was in when I reached there. I was soaking wet, but the rations were worse. Well, anyhow, I had to do my sentry duty, just the same, because if one man was shy those days it put all the work on some of his comrades. I could not get a change of clothing, so I took off my pants and wore my blanket like a Scotchman would his kilts. It's wonderful to me the hardships a man can contend with. We could get very little water up the front line and water means an awful lot to a man over there. Well, there was a creek running from the German front line across No Man's Land and into our trench, and coming over No Man's Land it ran over quite a few dead bodies. We were told by our medical officer not to drink this water because the Huns might have put poison into it. But we had to get water some place, so we all took a chance and drank it, and I am still alive and just as good as ever.

We were in the trenches for six days at a time. What good times we used to have when we were out in our billets. It was there we used to get the chance to have a good feed from the Belgian peasants. "Eggs and chips" was our favorite dish. Even when the men are out of the trenches they have to be ready in case of an attack. One night we got the orders from the front line that the trenches had caved in and of course we had to go up and help the boys build them up again.

It was this night, while carrying up sand bags, a bullet struck my right arm. I made the front line all right, but as soon as I was dressed by the stretcher bearer I was sent back to the dressing station to the medical officer to receive attention. I was then sent to the field hospital, and the next day I was removed on an ambulance train, and sent to the base hospital in Etaples. I might state that this hospital was an American hospital. How wonderful it was to me to find myself back in a nice white bed again. I was there for two weeks and then sent to a convalescent hospital for another week.

At the beginning of December I found myself on the way back to the front line. Of course all my pals who were still there were glad to see me again; but, believe me, it was hard to leave that nice white bed and go back "somewhere in the mud." I made the best of it. I knew it was doing my duty, as every soldier does.

I had quite a few narrow escapes after that. One day as I sat in the trench a German high explosive shell hit the next bay to where I was and when they explode they throw up with them all loose stuff that is in their reach. This one threw up an old French bayonet which missed my head by about two inches, but as long as it did not hit me I should worry.

Our routine there was, six days in the front line, six in the billets, and six in the reserve. The only thing I did not like about the reserve was, that the poor fellows that got killed in the trenches, if there was anything left of them to give a decent burial, were brought out of the trenches at night and put into an old barn near the dressing station until the next morning for burial. It was our duty to watch the bodies so that the rats would not eat them. Just imagine, about six fellows lying in an old barn all riddled with bullets and shrapnel, and the wind blowing, and the rain coming through, and to go and look at these poor fellows with a flash light. Some with their heads and arms blown off—but we had to do it.

From Kemmel Hill we were moved in March, 1916, to St. Eloi, where we put up a good scrap against heavy odds. I pulled through that all right. I remember we took some prisoners. There was a little Scotchman in my company who was always looking for souvenirs and he brought a big German down the trench and made a grab for his hat. The Dutchman made a grab for it and said:

"If you want to catch a cold, I don't."

I thought that was very funny, but Jock did not.

From there we moved to the Somme and it was here that the first British tanks were used. I got it again on the morning of September 15 from a German high explosive, was buried, receiving shell-shock and some wounds. A few days later found myself in a hospital and had a wonderful time, but I found that the doctors would not let me go back to France, so I was returned to Canada.

I was in Canada two weeks when I came over to the good old U. S. A. to help recruiting for the British and Canadian Army. I have worked on the Liberty Loan drives, Red Cross, Knights of Columbus, and all other drives to keep the boys over there. One thing, to my sorrow, during the Fourth Liberty Loan drive was that I sold all the buttons of my overcoat to each person who bought a five-hundred-dollar bond. The only thing that worried me was that I never had enough buttons, but as we all know a fellow would not want to have two or three hundred buttons on his coat to fasten. I only wish I was in France to stay to the finish, and come back with the rest of the boys who are left.

A "DEVIL DOG'S" STORY

By Pvt. Al. Barker, No. 118, 43d Company,
5th Regiment, U. S. Marines

THE U. S. declared war upon Germany April 6, 1917. I was going to college at the time. I went to spend a week-end in New York City and happened to be in Union Square where recruiting of soldiers, sailors, and marines was taking place. A captain of the U. S. Navy was speaking on patriotism. As I stood there and listened a thrill went through me and I decided to enlist at once. I chose the marines because they were always the "first to fight." I was sent to Paris Island, South Carolina, for my training, where I spent three months, and on August 12, 1917, I was sent to Quantico, Va., for my overseas equipment. On August 21, 1917, I sailed for France.

The trip across was a very eventful one, as we were twice shot at by submarines, but we succeeded in eluding them. Nine days later we arrived at Brest, France, where we were all stationed in barracks. My first real training began in France; drilled from morning to night, together with such things as trench digging, bayonet fighting, grenade throwing, and all other things necessary to an American marine. This lasted about three months. My first real encounter occurred when we were ordered to the Belgian Front with Australian

Anzacs. There I had my first glimpse of the Germans. We battled with them for twelve hours and I received a bayonet thrust in my right foot which laid me up for three weeks, and I was sent to base hospital No. 3 near St. Lazarre. After I recovered I was again sent to the Belgian Front where, in the next encounter with the Germans, I was captured and sent to a prison camp, built in the German trenches. I was there with eight other marines, for twenty-one days, when a French air squadron descended upon the Germans and killed or wounded all of them. A French aviator—I do not recall his name—took me in his machine and we flew 102 miles to the French forces.

Being weak from loss of blood and sleep I was kept there a week, and then sent back to my own company. My fellow-marines had given me up for dead, and were more than overjoyed to see me. A few days later I was selected as a sniper with a few others, and we advanced to a point as near the Germans as possible. Together with another marine, Jack Kneeland, who later saved my life, I climbed a tall tree as near as possible to the German trenches and stationed myself there very comfortably.

We could see the Germans setting machine guns in position to be used against our forces. We both had our rifles and plenty of ammunition, so we began to pick off the men who were operating the machine guns. These machine guns are the most disastrous and dangerous things in warfare. We succeeded in putting four of these guns out of commission when we were discovered by German snipers, and had all we could do to defend ourselves. I received a bullet wound in my knee and fell twenty feet to the ground. The other marine,

Kneeland, quickly descended and protected me with his own body, and although he received three bullets he carried me to safety. As we were far from any hospital we were treated in the trenches to the best of the abilities of the doctors there.

We had Germans all around us, and, although we kept up a heavy fire, we could not persuade them to come out and fight us as men. They preferred trying a means to defeat us which insured their own safety, and that was to try to starve us out. For six days we lived on hard black bread and dirty water. Our commander, previous to this, had sent out a marine, who had volunteered, to get through the German lines and bring us help. We never dreamed that he would succeed in getting through, but on the seventh day we saw several black specks in the air but thought nothing of them until they came close, and we saw that they were American airplanes come to our assistance. The fliers descended as low as possible and threw us food in water-proof canvas bags. They also dropped bombs on the Germans and then flew away after promising to send a company of marines to our rescue. This promise we found in a note contained in one of the bags of food. It also told us to keep up our courage, as we would surely be saved. All this time I was laid up with the wound in my knee, but I could hear our boys firing at the enemy, and they had all they could do to keep me in bed. Five days later I was aroused by an attendant and was told that an American scout had succeeded in making his way into our trenches, and told us that our relief was on its way, and would be here at any time. I felt much stronger after I heard this news and felt that I could fight the biggest German and finish him.

The detachment of marines arrived after we had been in these trenches for sixteen days. We now outnumbered the Germans, so we speedily put them to flight. After the conflict we counted 421 German dead bodies and we also took 1,200 prisoners. Our loss was sixty-two dead and thirty slightly wounded. We were then sent to a rest camp where we spent two weeks, and I had my wound treated. At the end of our two weeks I was able to walk about, and was sent to the western front near Cambrai where the Germans were gaining, and we were instructed to stop them.

This time we did not fight from the trenches but in the open field, and there were plenty of human targets for both sides. It was a terrible battle; shells were bursting in the air, cannons were roaring, and there were loud reports every time a shell hit the dust. I was operating a machine gun, and, as a machine gunner's life on a battlefield only lasted an average of twelve minutes, it must have been a miracle that saved me from being killed. My other two comrades were killed immediately and I was left alone to operate the gun. A German sniper took a shot at me, but instead of hitting me he put my gun out of order. That left me with only a revolver, and drawing this I kept popping away at every German I saw. At last we were given the order to advance and for the third time I went "Over the Top" to glory. As we pressed on the enemy gave way little by little, and by twelve o'clock, at noon (the battle had started the day before at the same hour), we had either killed or taken all our opponents prisoners. We were then given a much needed rest. We spent a month in a rest camp and were then sent to Chateau-Thierry, about forty miles from Paris, where we engaged in a battle which proved to be the turning-point of the war. I think I shall remember this fight all my life. We had drawn up all our ammunition trains, food supplies, and other munitions and were gathered around our campfires telling stories. At a little past midnight we were told to get ready. I was in the second division and we were ordered to advance first. Suddenly someone fired a shot; whether it came from our lines or the enemy I did not know. The battle had begun. With two hundred others I was cut off, and we found ourselves surrounded by the enemy. It was all hand-to-hand fighting, and more than once I felt a hand creep to my neck, or a cold blade touch my face, but always managed to ward it off. Five hours of hard fighting still found us in the midst of the Germans. Whispering a few words to my nearest companion, we made a dash and cut our way through the thick masses of the enemy. Having no cover, we gathered together the bodies of German dead and piled them one upon the other and used them as protection against our enemies. While here a gas bomb exploded and I fell back unconscious. When I came to myself I was aboard a ship bound for the good old U. S. A. As I was so badly gassed that I would no longer be useful as a fighter, they were sending me *home*. I made a good recovery and I thank God for my life.

That is my story, and if I had to go through it again I would do it gladly for my country and the flag.

IN THE VERDUN SECTOR

*By Corp. Frank J. Sears, Co. A,
9th Infantry, 2d Div., A.E.F.*

IN THE winter of 1917 we found ourselves marching along a little road somewhere in France. It was cold and dismal and the hail came down in sheets, but we marched on and on. I looked at the fellow alongside of me and could not tell whether he was ready to laugh or cry. There was not much talking en route. I didn't feel much like talking myself and couldn't understand what made me feel so downhearted. It was the day we all looked and hoped for our chance in the battle. When we took over our sector, one kilometer from St. Mihiel, the French told us it was a quiet sector and to keep it that way. The first four days we did not care how quiet it was so long as we were allowed down in the dugouts. The shells whizzing past our heads annoyed us a little, it being our first experience. It took us a few days to become accustomed to our new home and the noise of bursting shrapnel. We knew we were not going to stay there long. In the American Army we never do linger long in one place, as there is no retreat in our army.

There was only one direction for us to follow and that was toward Berlin.

The idea of the French telling us to keep Verdun sector quiet amused us, for, while we had no desire to start anything for a few days, there wasn't a "yellow" man in our bunch. Yet we hesitated, before we became accustomed to the noise, to take our first chance at, what we termed, slaughter. However, one night, about seven days after we took over our sector with the French Army, a "Fritz" sent over one of his 77 shrapnel shells which wiped out our entire mess shack. That was a bad mistake on "Fritzie's" part for it was a serious offense for anybody to tamper with the Sammie's "chow." No matter how hard a night he has spent he will always get up an appetite where there is anything to eat. That night we formed a raiding party. We crept out of the first line trench with three squads. It was our first entry into No Man's Land and we had heard so many strange tales about this place, we shied at everything we saw. We split up into squads. Our password was to knock three times on the helmet. So we parted. I went off to the right with a squad. Each man covered his ground, trying to find out whether the Hun had any intention of making a raid next day. The trenches are protected by barbed-wire fences and when the Huns intend going "Over the Top" they cut the wires on the previous night, and it was our duty to find out whether or not these wires had been cut. The barbed wire was O. K. on the ground we covered, so we started back to meet the other squads. We did not go far, for about ten feet away we heard a noise, which is something unusual on a raiding party in No Man's Land. We stopped short and looked at each other. We did not know what to do, for, as I have said, this was our first experience. One of the boys said to me, "Give them the signal." I knocked three times on my helmet, but received no reply, so one of the boys said he would creep over and investigate; but it wasn't necessary, because just then a skyrocket went up into the air. Every soldier knows that this means to get under cover quickly for the rocket would light up the sky and make nice targets of us for "Fritz." Luckily for us there was a shell-hole to jump into, for as soon as we laid low, there came the "pop," "pop," "pop" of the German machine guns. We laid there in the mud, through what seemed to us like an eternity, but which was in reality only about two hours. However, luck was with us, and we finally crawled out of our hiding place and arrived behind our own lines once more.

EDITOR'S NOTE.—*For his gallantry in this raid, of which he says nothing in the above article, Corporal Sears was awarded the "Croix de Guerre" by the French Government.*
—*H. L. F.*

THE HUN I WAS SURE I "GOT"

By Corp. Frank J. Sears

IT WAS sometime last April, 1918, when we got the order we were going over. Our artillery opened up with a full barrage. We took the right flank, and another regiment of infantry took the left. The marines took the center. We had been told time and time again if we had to use the bayonet to pull it out quick. But somehow or other I was doubtful about that. We were having a real American hand-to-hand fight with them when I got my eye on one, something we very seldom do. Just as I got near him he threw his gun down, and his hands up, and yelled: "Kamerad, Kamerad." I said "Kamerad, hell," and became so excited I gave him a long jab with my old American bayonet and hesitated before making an attempt to pull it out. When I tried to, it was too late for it was wedged in too firmly. I put my foot on him and pulled and pulled, but the body lifted right up with the bayonet, so I thought I'd try my luck without a bayonet. I released the bayonet from my rifle and left it as an American souvenir to the "Fritz"; one which he will never be able to appreciate. This is all I remember of that battle.

LIFE IN THE TRENCHES

By Corp. Frank Sears

LIFE in the trenches is made up of "cooties," "rats," "mud," and "gas masks."

We had heard from fellows who had been there before us what we thought were jokes about "cooties" and trench rats, but it was no joke to me when I looked, for the first time, at a rat almost as big as a cat. It was lying in my bunk and I heard it squeal. Looking down I had my first view of a trench rat. I threw a heavy hob-nailed shoe at him and he merely changed his position and looked around to see who had interrupted him. After that it wasn't strange to wake up and find them running across you. But I will say that if it were a matter of choice, I would select a hundred rats in preference to two "cooties," for the "cootie" is an unreasonable bird, and when a Sammie has come back from the lines exhausted, he lays down in the hopes of snatching a few hours' sleep before being called on; but the "cooties" have no respect for Sammie and they pester him until he has no more idea of sleep, only to start in and hunt for the "cooties" that are annoying him.

You have all more or less had fever, but I guess there are none of you, over here, who knows of the "mud fever." We all used to shy at mud, during the rainy season in the year 1917. After a heavy storm the boys hated to go out to drill, as the mud got so bad there that the only way of getting out from the drill was by going on sick report in the morning. I remember the morning six buddies and myself went over to the infirmary. I happened to be the first one in line. The doctor came up to me and said:

"What's your trouble?"

At first I said, "I don't know, sir," and he said:

"Well, what are you doing here if you don't know? Where do you feel sick?"

And I told him all over. So he called the pill roller over and told him to take my temperature. I sat down and the pill roller put the glass tube in my mouth, which always "balled the detail up." He then held hands with me for a while and I asked him what he was doing. He told me he was taking my pulse. He then gave the final report to the "skipper" who came to me and said, "You have the 'mud fever.'" He then turned to the orderly and said, "Give him two C.C. pills and mark him 'DUTY.'" That's how I happened to get over the mud fever. We became so used to mud, up in the lines, that if our "chow" did not have some mud, or muddy water, in it we could not digest it. It was just a case of mud all over: eat, drink, sleep, and wash in mud.

And now for the "old reliable," which tortured us while wearing it, but without which we should have been lost. The gas mask!!!

We were not fortunate enough to have ever received the American gas masks and have never seen one over there. The first two American divisions received English and French masks. The English mask looks like a false face with two big glass eyes, and a nose clip which resembles a clothespin, and keeps the gas from going through the nostrils. There is also a tube which goes into the mouth, with a hard piece of rubber on it to make it air-tight. This mouthpiece is a long caterpillar tube which connects the mask to a tin can containing a chemical composition of charcoal, rocks, sand, and other medical decoctions. There were times when we endured these masks from eighteen to thirty-six hours. Sometimes we would just get the order to take them off, and, thinking the danger passed, would get ready to eat, when the command to put them on again would be given. This is done by means of horns at intervals along the whole line of trenches. Each horn gives the signal which is repeated right through the lines. It is a wonderful relief after having a mask on a long time to be able to breathe fresh air again.

TWO YEARS IN THE YPRES SALIENT

As Told by Private Albert Franklin Edwards, No. 6857, 1st Battalion, 1st Brigade, 1st Div., Canadian Infantry

EDITOR'S NOTE.—*These were the first Canadians to go overseas in the Great War.*

—H. L. F.

I WAS born in Canada, but had lived virtually all my life in the United States. I thought war was coming and returned to Canada to be ready to do my bit when the time arrived; and I was just in time; arriving in Toronto on August 3, 1914. On August 4, 1914, I was at dinner with seven other boys when the word came that war was declared, and the whole eight of us determined to get in it without delay, so on the next day, August 5th, we enlisted in the Canadian dragoons.

After two weeks in the dragoons I was transferred to the infantry, went into training at Toronto, and afterward at Valcartier, which occupied the next two months.

One Sunday morning we were called for parade and thought we were going to church, but were notified we had to pack up for overseas service. We went to Montreal where we took a boat down the St. Lawrence to Halifax. We there joined the convoy consisting of 33,000 men of the artillery and infantry.

We sailed for England on October 22, 1914, and as nearly as I can remember took about sixteen days to make the trip to Plymouth. Though slow the voyage was without incident worthy of mention.

We were, for some unknown reason, held five days in Plymouth Harbor before disembarking, and then they hustled us off to the training camp on Salisbury Plains where we had a miserable existence until February, 1915.

At Salisbury we drilled in mud and water that was at times waist deep, caused by the continuous rains and floods. It sure was fine training for the Flanders mud that we were to encounter later. The storms were so severe at times that tents and their contents were washed away.

As a result an epidemic of spinal meningitis hit the camp, and of the 33,000 who arrived at Salisbury 4,400 were stricken with this disease, only a few of whom recovered.

While at Salisbury I was granted my first leave and started for London, together with my pal, a boy named Frazer, who also had leave. We had three days' absence from camp coming to us and they were "some three days."

We arrived in London at 5.15 P.M. and, in accord with English custom, had tea at once in the Corner House, Piccadilly, where many soldiers congregated.

At the Corner House we received sixty-one invitations to the theater and dinner for the next day. That night we attended the Princess Theater where, as we entered, the orchestra played the Canadian anthem, "The Maple Leaf

Forever." The audience cheered and we were forced to make a speech. You see, we were the first Canadians the English people had seen who had come to do their bit. That night I lost track of Frazer.

After three wonderful days I returned to camp as my leave had expired. Frazer was not on the train with me, and as a matter of fact did not arrive until twenty-four hours later. He was called before the colonel for overstaying his leave, and, on being questioned, told the colonel that just as he arrived at the railroad station a band started playing "God Save the King" and he had to stand at attention so long that he missed the train.

He was excused and returned to duty, but they do say there was a suspicious twinkle in the colonel's eye as he dismissed him. I sometimes wish I had Frazer's powers of quick invention.

On February 3rd we left Salisbury encampment, en route for France, landing at St. Lazarre, thence by train to Hazebrouck and St. Omer where the fever laid me up in the hospital for about ten days.

I joined the battalion again at Armentières where we remained a few days and then went forward to Ypres. On April 22, 1915, we went into battle at Ypres and for the first time in history were called upon to meet a gas attack by the Germans.

EDITOR'S NOTE.—This was the first time this inhuman method of warfare was used by a supposedly civilized nation.

H. L. F.

At first we thought the gas we saw coming toward us was a bank of fog and it gave us no anxiety. It was at 4.30 P.M. that the Huns turned the gas on us, and I was fortunate to be in the first battalion at a point where the gas was not so thick. The thickest part of the gas swept over the 8th, 10th, 11th, 13th, 14th, 15th, and 16th battalions. Eighty-five per cent of the men who met this attack were more or less severely gassed. At points the gas was so severe that it turned the brass buttons, on the tunics of the men, green. Some of the men killed by gas fell, but some remained standing even in death so swift was its action.

Our artillery, although short of ammunition, was our main support in this action. Had the Germans forced a passage here, the roads to Paris, Calais, and the English coast would have been virtually open. There were 72,000 Germans opposed to 13,000 Canadian infantry in this action, but the boys from Canada held fast.

The next day, April 23rd, a small fragment of shrapnel in my right hand sent me to the hospital in Boulogne. Fine treatment by the American doctors and nurses there soon had me in shape again and I was returned to the line through the Canadian base at Le Havre. Thence I went through Festubert to Givenchy where the old 1st Battalion went into battle with 919 men and six hours later over 600 had made the great sacrifice. Minor casualties left us only 137 men able to answer roll call and several of these had to go to the hospital on account of wounds received here.

The first week of July we went to Ploegsteert which we called "home" for a long time. We called Ploegsteert "home" because it was so peaceful. (The Germans dared not shell us, as we were so close to their trenches that they were afraid of hitting their own men.) The shell craters through which our trenches ran were only thirteen yards from the trenches of the enemy, and we could hear the Saxons who opposed us singing songs in English which they all seemed to speak fluently.

One night I was on patrol when our party passed a German patrol not five yards distant. Neither side dared fire for fear of starting the machine gun fire. One of the Saxons called out, "Hello, Canuck, how's Quebec, Winnipeg, and Vancouver?"

Evidently he had been in Quebec as he spoke of the St. Regis Hotel.

At Ploegsteert the British had started a "sap" forty-eight feet deep where a tunnel, with twenty-five galleries running off from it, undermined the town. It took two years to build and was planted with one hundred thousand tons of high explosive dynamite. When it was exploded it blew up the entire town and also blew 61,000 Huns "Hell, west, and crooked."

This was the only way to take the position, as the elaborate trench system of the Germans was practically impregnable. It was at Ploegsteert that the Huns "got our goat" by showing the wearing apparel of Belgian girls on the points of their bayonets.

After exploding the mine we explored the German trenches and found most wonderful underground living quarters for the troops fitted with every modern convenience.

We remained here three and a half months and then were moved to Kemmel to the C-4 trenches, where we spent the winter. Here I was taken sick and sent to the hospital at Bailleu, and returned to duty again at Cambrai, and thence went to St. Quentin.

Remained at St. Quentin until September 17th, when I had a piece of shrapnel lodge in my arm and was burned by a shell while trying to dig out a comrade in a similar predicament, except that he died before we got him out. I was buried, but conscious, for four hours and twenty minutes, and I thought of every event of my life in that time. When finally rescued, the fresh air and reaction were too much for me, and I lost consciousness, which I did not regain until I was in England in the Duchess of Connaught's Hospital. I had been sent there by way of Le Havre and remained six months in bed in a plaster cast. I was then returned to a hospital ship and taken to St. John, New Brunswick, where I received electrical and massage treatment. From St. John I went to the convalescent hospital at Fredericton, N. B., and was discharged on August 19, 1918.

A NIGHT ADVENTURE

*As Told by Private Albert Franklin Edwards,
No. 6857, 1st Battalion, 1st Brigade,
1st Division, Canadian Infantry*

ONE night in October, 1915, while on patrol, I found an officer, and a private, of the Prussian Guard, fooling around our wire entanglements. They had evidently been under our fire as the officer was suffering from three abdominal wounds and died as I was trying to drag him into our lines.

The private was a big fellow about six feet three inches tall and was furious at being captured. As I had him at my bayonet's point he gave me no trouble, but when we arrived at our lines he took it out on the sentry by spitting at him and slapping him in the face.

We sat Mr. Prussian on the firing step and told him a few things that would not look well in this book, and he finally spoke in English, when we called the escort to get what information we could from him. He asked after some friends he had made at Columbia College, New York City, where he had been educated. He told us that just before the war broke out he had been called back to Germany, supposedly to attend a military fête, as he was still subject to military service. He had no idea, he said, that he was going to be sent to war and he had been drugged and sent into battle, forced on by officers in the rear. After we had "pumped him dry" he was handed over, together with fourteen other prisoners, who were taken the same night, and sent to the cage, four miles to the rear. On the way to the cage he complained to a soldier, in the guard accompanying the prisoners, of the difficulty of marching through the mud, which was very deep. The guard told him he should be thankful that he was not in his (the guard's) place, as he had to walk back again.

I should have stated before that I cut off the buttons from the officer's uniform when he died and kept them together with his field glasses as souvenirs. I have them still, as no one has claimed them.

A MACHINE GUNNER'S STORY

*By Machine Gunner George Eckhart,
No. 165688, 1st M. G. Batt., 1st Div., A.E.F.*

I ENLISTED in the service of my country April 6, 1917, when we declared war on Germany. I was sent to Fort Douglas, Arizona, in the same month, put in the 18th Infantry, Regular Army.

On June 4, 1917, we got orders to pack up and leave for another camp, and one night when our train came to a halt I got up from bed and said to the boys:

"Boys, we are in Hoboken," and we all knew then where we were going.

We got on the transports the same night about eleven o'clock. There were a lot of sad faces watching their dear boys going "Over There" to fight to make the world safe for Democracy.

We sailed away from dear old America, June 14, 1917. When we passed the Statue of Liberty we watched her holding the light of freedom and strained our eyes as our transport moved out into the ocean for a last look at her, wondering if we would ever see that dear old Statue of Liberty again.

We had a pleasant, fourteen-day trip across the ocean. And one bright morning we saw land. All the boys shouted, "France, we have come to you." Four hours later we were beside our dock, and got off the boats. All the French people kissed us and were glad to see America come to help her sister republic.

The French people shouted, "Vive la America." We shouted back, "Vive la France." We had a big reception and the peasants took us around and showed us the villages.

We did not stay there long, but moved toward the front where we could hear the thundering of the artillery barrages. We had two months of strenuous training with the French Blue Devils.

After completing our training period we got orders that we were going to go to the Front. One day, before we left to undertake the biggest job in the world, our general (General Bullard) held an inspection, and gave us a talk.

He said, "Boys, you are going to tackle a real job tomorrow, and show the Huns what kind of stuff the Yanks are made of."

All of the boys yelled, "We are with you, general, until the end. We are going to give them hell! and, we won't go back until it's over, over here."

The next day we were ready to move to the Front. The colonel gave the command, and we marched off. We had to walk fifty miles.

As we came nearer and nearer to the front, the guns were roaring and machine guns rattled away like fire. The first division, consisting of the 18th Infantry, 26th Infantry, 16th, and 18th Infantry, started to sing, "Hail, Hail, the Gang's All

Here!" At last we arrived at the Front. Our French comrades hailed us, and were surprised and overjoyed to see the Yanks coming to relieve them and give them a rest.

Company after company moved in and relieved the French division and as they moved out they bid us all the luck in the world.

This front was the Lorraine front, Luneville Sector. The next day, October 14, 1917, our artillery fired the first shells into the German trenches.

The Germans got kind of restless and wondered who was facing them. They sent out a patrolling party to gather information. But we boys were a little too wise and our patrol party captured this German party and brought them in. When they came in our trenches they asked us who we were. I spoke up and said, "We are Americans," and the German officer who spoke a little English said, "No! No! you are not an American. You are English in American uniforms." But they soon found out that we *were* Americans and we did "treat 'em rough!"

I was now transferred to a machine gun company and was on duty one night about 11.30. It was very cold. My loader Frank Martin and I were talking quietly about our dear homes across the sea. Suddenly the German machine guns opened up and we ducked down in our own gun emplacement and could hear the bullets hissing over our heads. Then it was silent again. We knew the Huns were getting restless, so our signal captain sent up a "very light" which lights up No Man's Land. And we saw about 5,000 Prussian guards coming at us with bayonets fixed. I held fast to my trigger, waiting for orders.

The lieutenant came to me and said, "George, don't get nervous. We are going to get them in a trap." And I said:

"Lieutenant, do you think I will ever see the Statue of Liberty again?"

He said, "Cheer up, George, I will send the order soon."

So they fired another "very light" and there they were 100 yards from where I was stationed. All was quiet. We kept still as mice.

Then suddenly a big red rocket went up which called for an artillery barrage and I heard the shells of our artillery firing behind the Germans so they could not go back to their own lines. This was followed by two red rockets, meaning direct fire from our own machine guns. And then I yelled, "Here's where the suicide club shines," and opened up.

We gave them all the "presents" they wanted. My machine gun was red hot, and my hands were burning, but I didn't mind that. We were going to get them and give them what they deserved.

We gave them "sweeping fire" and mowed them down like grass. Daylight came and there were the Prussian Guards in big piles, dead and wounded. We certainly did catch them in a trap.

That morning I went into the dugout and we boys sat around on bundles of straw and sang some songs and told stories and jokes.

When the mail man would come around with the letters from home, we would gather around him and listen for our names to be called.

The boys that got letters from their dear mothers had smiles on their faces and were happy, knowing their mothers were thinking of them. And those that didn't get letters were sad and disgusted and would have tears rolling down their cheeks.

We stayed on that front two months. Christmas was on its way, and we went back for a rest. At Christmas time all the boys gave ten francs (two dollars, U. S. money) to give the little children of France a real American Christmas.

After six days of preparation, we went to the Salvation Army hut and had a big entertainment. Elsie Janis was the chief entertainer. After the entertainment was over we all returned to bed.

The next day the church bells rang out and the little children ran about wild with joy. The Yankee soldiers gave the children candy, cakes, pies, and other little presents and they could not get over it, as they never had a Christmas like that before.

EDITOR'S NOTE.—The simple pathos of this story so appealed to me, that, knowing no words of mine could so vividly depict the feelings of this hero, I have given it to the readers of the book without revision. I simply desire to add that the action which he describes in the above story was the first of the Great War participated in by American Troops.

H. L. F.

THE FALL OF CANTIGNY

By Machine Gunner George Eckhart

BEFORE proceeding with my second story, I wish to state that Cantigny Village was the first town ever captured by the American troops in this war, and also the first battle we ever had. My division, the "First," known all over France as the "Black Jack" Division, was named after General "Black Jack" Pershing.

After leaving Lorraine front and spending Christmas behind the lines, we were ordered to a more active front in Picardy, where some of the biggest battles have taken place during this Great War.

We relieved the 2nd French Colonial Division and took over their sector. We faced the town Cantigny, which is situated twenty miles northwest of Montdidier.

This town was hard to take, as there were two Prussian Guard divisions against one Yankee division.

Our general said, "Boys, we are going to take that town and we will take it inside of seventy-two hours." Us boys all felt proud and were ready to go "Over the Top" any time the order came.

Jimmy Doyle, the loader on my machine gun, was the youngest boy in the battalion, and he was kind of nervous when he knew we were going "Over the Top" in seventy-two hours. He sat down in the dugout, writing a letter to his dear mother, with the shells and shrapnel going over our heads. He expected a letter from his mother for three months but never received it.

So Little Jimmie put in his letter, "Mother, I am writing you this letter and it may be the last as I am going 'Over the Top' for the first time, and I am going to do my bit even if I am only seventeen years old. I wrote you ten letters and you have not written me one, so mother, dear, please write your little Jimmie a letter. Good Bye and God bless you. Jimmie."

The seventy-two hours had come and it was growing dark. We had extra ammunition stacked beside our machine gun, ready to open fire on the Huns. "Little Jimmie" worked hard stacking up the ammunition. The infantry was "standing to" waiting for the word.

Everything was quiet. We had five minutes to think of our people back home. "Little Jimmie" said to me:

"George, you were one of my best friends. I am a kid, but if I get killed, tell my mother I died for her and the Stars and Stripes."

The time had come and the French tanks had started their engines. The red rocket went up. Our artillery laid down their barrage and we opened rapid fire with our machine guns. "Little Jimmie" was feeding the gun like a veteran.

Shells were whistling all around us. The captains of all infantry companies yelled, "Over the Top with the best of luck and give them Hell. Up and at 'em, boys!"

And when they went over the boys yelled and cheered, rushing onward to the Hun trenches, "Remember the

Lusitania," "Remember the *Antilles*," "Remember the U. S.," "Remember dear President Wilson and the Stars and Stripes."

They kept on gaining, facing death and danger. We followed them up with our machine guns. The Huns started with their artillery. They thought they could stop us but they couldn't. We always had our fighting spirit with us.

The German Prussian Guards came over to meet us. Our infantry went at 'em, facing them. Some yelled, "Kamerad," but that didn't go with us. We gave them the cold steel instead. We had 500 yards to go to before we could take Cantigny. "Little Jimmie" Doyle was working hard at the gun and he would say, "I wonder if my mother is thinking of me." We kept moving our gun and giving them all they wanted. All of a sudden "Little Jimmie" fell with a Hun machine gun bullet through his head. The blood was pouring down his cheek. I went to him, gave him my first aid packet with bandages, put it around his head,—but in vain. He was taking his last breath. He said:

"George, good bye, I knew this was my day."

He wanted to say a few more words, but could not. He lay still without breathing. He was dead, and he died with a smile on his lips. The poor lad was always happy and had a smile for whoever he met. "Little Jimmie" died for his country and died like a man.

After taking Jimmie away I ran back to my machine gun. The Prussians were coming over, driving back the infantry. They overpowered us but the machine gunners all said: "We are going to hold this line until the infantry gets reinforcements." We eight machine gunners were checking the Germans finally. Now and then we stopped firing. Then the Huns would rush at us, thinking that they had killed us, but we were very much alive and as soon as they advanced a hundred yards or so, we would open up our machine guns again and give 'em Hell. Four of the machine gunners were killed and it was up to the remaining four to hold them back until the infantry came.

Our ammunition was getting low and I was shot through my leg by a high explosive shrapnel, but I kept on with my machine gun until our infantry came up with the reinforcements, and went over with a yell and chased the Huns back and captured Cantigny. We got that town in two and a half hours.

My leg was bleeding and I had an awful pain but I stuck to it. We went into the Hun trenches, which we had captured, and there I was treated by the Red Cross dressing station and then we went in and brought out the German prisoners who were hiding in the dugouts and cellars of the town.

Then the Germans, who were driven back to their reserve trenches, wanted to get square on us, and fired over the poisonous gas. We got the signal and put our masks on, and kept them on for seventy-two hours. Mine was an old mask and it began to leak, until suddenly I fell, and was unconscious for twenty-four hours. When I awoke I was in the hospital, in a nice white bed such as I had not been in for ten months. Oh! didn't I sleep. They couldn't get me up for anything.

I was nursed back to health, and, when I went back to the front, they had a great surprise for me. I was summoned to

General Headquarters and there I was awarded the French war cross, or "Croix de Guerre," for heroism during the battle of Cantigny. We all sang the song of songs, "Over There," by the Yankee Doodle Boy, George M. Cohan. We used this song all the time when we would march into battle, and sang it again when we came out victorious.

Then I was sent home to dear America and my people were more than pleased to see me march in a hero from "Over There."

Then they had me talking for the Knights of Columbus drive, Liberty Loan, also the United War Work Campaign. The American people may well be proud when their sons and sweethearts come marching home victorious,—as they all fought well to make the world safe and a decent place to live in.

THE RETREAT FROM MONS

By Sergt. T. S. Grundy

I WAS one of the first 100,000 men of British Expeditionary Force sent to Belgium in August, 1914. The great retreat from Mons and the different battles (rearguard actions) that took place afterward were some of the worst and fiercest actions that the British Forces ever fought. Of course we know that not so many guns were used and nothing like the barrage that is put down nowadays, but it was hard and severe fighting with hardships that are no longer necessary today. The Lewis machine gun, and the new types today, were not known then. We went to the field with the old Maxim type used in previous warfare. Such was the equipment of the first 100,000 men of the British Expeditionary Forces. Our forces were spread out on a twenty-two-mile front. Just a mere handful of men that, without a doubt, saved Europe from Prussian rule; although thousands do not realize this. If the enemy had known of the weakness of our forces he would have walked across Belgium and France. However, the enemy underestimated our forces, and the stubborn and determined fight of, what the Kaiser called, England's "Contemptible Little Army" saved the situation. At Mons it was a case of, if the enemy broke through the line, there were no reserves to bring up, so, officer and man alike, we stood to the last. When the enemy broke through in certain parts of the lines—then came the hard fighting. "Fritz" would break through on the left flank and endeavor to cut us off, then came the time man after man went down, and, slowly, we had to retreat assisted by cavalry, against, literally speaking, hordes and hordes of Germany's best soldiers. Some companies were not so fortunate, being completely surrounded, and annihilated, or taken prisoners, very few escaping to tell the tale, and those that escaped to the woods had no rations, and lived like savages, on anything that could be found.

Unfortunately not many of these men are alive today, being afterward captured by the enemy and killed by ill-treatment in internment camps, or starved to death in the woods. It was when the retreat was looking very serious, and no reserves forthcoming, that the most wonderful and thrilling incidents of the war occurred, and this is vouched for by all who were there. When comrades were falling, one after the other, and the Germans advancing in great masses, Angels appeared from the skies and seemed to stop the approach of the enemy. They appeared to fall back temporarily in sheer disorder. This was only a temporary collapse, but it gave time for better preparations on our part, and this is what saved us from being wiped out, as reserves were forthcoming afterward. An incident of the enemy's method of warfare by unscrupulous means came to my notice. We would not have lost half of the men we did, at Mons, if it had not been for this. It was the fault of a French colonel who was under the influence of his wife, a German woman, a spy of the German empire, and she so used her influence over her husband that he kept back two or three regiments of reserves for three days, under the pretext of resting them, when they might have been up and probably saved the situation. This colonel was afterward court-martialed and shot, Lord Kitchener coming from England to investigate this.

Our enemy, as we have seen all through the war, has used these unscrupulous methods. We lost 60,000 out of 100,000 1st B. E. F. Over half our army was taken prisoners, killed, and wounded. Out of my battalion there were twenty-eight survivors—I being one of them.

After Mons came the great battle of Ypres, in which our regiment took part. Things were nearly always very brisk in this sector of the line. I remember one particular night, my chum and I were out on listening posts when my chum thought he saw the enemy advancing. I looked and could not see them. He started making a row, and I warned him to be quiet, but he didn't heed me, when suddenly he went down mortally wounded. I dived to the ground, and in diving my hands came in contact with a man who had probably been dead some days. This was not an unusual occurrence. About Sept. 15th, when we were up at Ypres again, there was a party of us who went on a bombing raid one night. Nearly every night a bombing party went out into No Man's Land. At this particular time, however, we were returning from a bombing raid, perhaps without as much caution as usual, when a shell burst right among us, killing every man except myself and a chum, who was badly wounded. I, however, found I had escaped with but a few scratches, and taking along my chum who had a bad wound in the leg, managed, after much trouble, to return to our lines. My chum, not being able to walk, made it difficult for me. I had to carry him back, and to look out for "whizz-bangs," and avoid tumbling into shell-holes. The weather at this time of the year was very bad; raw and cold weather, up to our knees in mud and water, stuck in the trenches, day after day, and week after week. Such is trench life in winter time. But when springtime came again, then things started to "liven up." "Fritz" was at it again. Our battalion was up at Ypres salient, where a terrific artillery duel was being put up at the time. Shells were dropping all around, star-shells illuminated the skies, and the word was passed around for getting ready to go "Over the Top."

It was dawn, and, the rum ration having been handed around, the order was given, and over we went. Some were just up and over and down they went. I remember our captain was one of the first to fall. His words as he fell were: "Carry on, boys, don't mind me," and the boys carried on. All I could see before me was blood. It seemed as if I had no other object in mind but to kill. Such were my feelings as we went over. We hadn't advanced above 300 yards when a bullet whizzed too close for my liking, and, turning my head, I saw my chum fall, and dozens of others, but our orders were "carry on," and get our objective. Next our first lieutenant fell and mustering us together, our remaining lieutenant, a mere youth of eighteen years, and a small handful of men, reached our position, not without severe loss of life. I remember one little incident. A German officer lying severely wounded, called in almost perfect English for a drink. One of the boys (probably a little more human than some of us) went to give him a drink out of his water bottle. Then the

Prussian officer drew his revolver and shot this boy. Those who witnessed the incident, I being among them, made short work of the Prussian beast, but this incident goes to show the Prussians' hate of his enemy.

The Saxon troops are the most civilized of the bunch. An incident of just the opposite, I witnessed down at the Somme. A wounded German soldier called for water to drink and one of our Tommies kindheartedly went and gave it to him. They conversed for a minute or two. The German spoke in broken English. He said to the Tommy, as he undid his tunic and displayed a Salvation Army jersey, "I am a Salvationist," and the British Tommy replying said, "So am I." They shook hands and the German fell back dead. Never shall I forget the sights that I have seen in the trenches we took from the Boches. I remember one particular trench we took, we found a young girl about nineteen years of age, who had one of her eyes taken out, an ear cut off, and her right breast severed. This was not an isolated case of the Boche's villainy. I personally witnessed, in villages in France and Belgium, the bodies of old men that had been crucified or slowly tortured to death. I have seen a little baby bayonetted to a doorpost and the bayonet left sticking in the body.

It was down at Loos that I was gassed. I have a recollection of the gas coming over and was unconscious for twenty-four hours, and had oxygen pumped into me. When I returned to consciousness I found myself in a hospital with a Red Cross nurse bending over me. Another sector of the line I was in was at Cambrai (after my recovery from the hospital). Here we caught it pretty rough. It was the time that British divisions were being drafted off to Italy that things were lively. Several battalions were being marched off to Italy, when "Fritz" broke through part of our line down south, and advanced in mass formation. Then we were ordered to retreat. It was some retreat! Guns were left, ammunition dumps not blown up, and we retreated about thirty miles. Our losses there were great. However, in small counter-attacks and skirmishes, which our battalion took part in, we captured quite a few prisoners. I was quite surprised to notice how young some of these German soldiers seemed—not more than seventeen years of age. In the early part of 1918 I was up in Ypres again where one night we had after severe fighting recaptured a few hundred yards. I was just standing around in the captured trenches, when a shell burst and a piece of shrapnel caught me. Down I went, to awake once more in a hospital, where the boys were all content and happy, in spite of wounds. So was I, especially when I heard I was for "Blighty" once again.

MY SERVICE IN FLANDERS

By Sergt. Alexander Gibb, No. 444476,
Co. A. 26th Batt., N. B. Regt., Canadian Inf.

IN THE month of October, 1914, the second Canadian Division was being formed. I being too young at that time, could not enlist, but in the month of February, 1915, I did enlist with the 55th Battalion. The commander of that battalion was Lieutenant Colonel Kirkpatrick. It was in the month of March of the same year that our regiment went into camp at Sussex, N. B. Every day of our life in camp was work, day and night, but of course our battalion found time for their sports; even if we did have to work very hard during the day.

In the beginning of June of that year there was a call came to our regiment for volunteers to go overseas, with the 26th Battalion, which is now known as the Famous Fighting 26th; at that time under command of Lieutenant Colonel McAvity, better known as "Colonel Jim." Of course I was eager to get over and do my bit. I was one of the many who volunteered. It was on the most unlucky day of that month, June 13, 1915, that the 26th sailed on the transport *Caledonian* for an unknown port in England. As the transport moved from the pier amid cheering crowds, the boys were happy and gay.

Our voyage across the pond was uneventful, only we were all given life belts which we had to wear all the time of our trip, and of course we had our life boat drill, which took place in the morning after our physical training. The afternoon was spent in sports of all kinds, boxing, running, etc. We did not come in contact with any U-boats and I might say we had very little seasickness on board. Our trip of nine days was the most enjoyable trip I have ever had on the water. When we were a few miles from our landing place, away off in the distance we could see two destroyers coming toward us. At first we thought they were "Fritzies" but as they came nearer we found them to be British destroyers coming to escort us into the harbor at Southampton.

On arriving at that port, amid cheering crowds, we disembarked for our training camp in England. We marched to the station and boarded the train. At every step we made, the English people would give us hot tea, cake, and fruit, and we sure did enjoy it.

We arrived in the City of Folkestone, and from there marched to the training camp, known as West Sandling camp. We were tired out from our long train journey, and had a quiet repose in our new home. Our training started in real earnest there. A lot of it was quite new to us, such as musketry, bayonet fighting, trench warfare, bombing, etc. After two months of hard work, and long marches, the word came at last for us to show the Huns what we were made of. We received orders for parade in full marching order—then were marched about five miles to the transport, which was waiting for us at Folkestone. I might say that was in the month of September, 1915. Our voyage across the channel was very rough, but of course we did not mind it.

We arrived in the city of Boulogne, on the coast of France, and marched from there to a rest camp, staying there for three days. Once more we got orders to move on. We marched about forty or forty-five miles to St. Omer, then on to a rest camp behind the lines at Kemmel Hill, which is in Flanders.

After a brief rest, our battalion went into the front line, at the above mentioned place. As we were nearing the front lines we could hear the big guns and shells bursting overhead; also the whistling of bullets. Of course, I naturally started ducking my head, and I have been ducking ever since. In the week of the 12th of October, our battalion was in the front line, in the P. E. O. trenches at Kemmel, and on that day "Fritzie" sprung a mine in No Man's Land which formed a big crater. On the morning of the 13th we got orders that we were to take that crater. The time set for going "Over the Top" was 2 A.M. and every man was ready and eager to show what he was made of. To the minute a blast of the whistle came, and we were over. "Fritzie" saw us and he also came over. Then a hand-to-hand fight started. I came in contact with a big Hun, and of course we went to it. Before many seconds had passed, I got his bayonet over the bridge of the nose, but it did not knock me out, and a short time after I got him; my first Hun. My, but I was a proud boy. I put my hand to my face and it became covered with blood—so I started back to the trench to get my wound dressed. On arriving at my battalion dressing station the doctor started operations. He put four stitches in my nose and then I was sent back to a field hospital for further treatment. While at the hospital

I heard that our battalion had taken the crater and covered itself with glory, but our losses were heavy. It was during that fight that my regiment made itself famous.

After two weeks in the hospital, I was sent back to my regiment which was in a rest camp. I carried back with me two lovely black eyes from the effect of the wound.

Once more we moved into the trenches, under a heavy downpour of rain. The winter had just set in. It was cold and damp under foot, and the water reached up to our knees. During our stay in the line at that time, I recall an incident which happened. I was sitting in a dugout, having a bite to eat with some of my pals, and enjoying the meal quite well. Something had to spoil our lunch, of course. A shell came over and burst on top of the dugout and buried us for about four or five hours. We were in darkness—then we were dug out, and were none the worse from our little experience.

MY SERVICE IN FLANDERS

Part Two
By Sergt. A. Gibb

DURING our stay in the line at Kemmel Hill, after the crater fight, the winter started in real earnest. The snow and sleet was something awful. Nothing but wet feet all the time. Had it not been for our rum ration, we should have died from disease. A great number of our boys did die. Some of the boys in our working party who went up the line, while we were in billets, were drowned in the shell-holes, that were filled with water, or got trench feet and were sent to the hospital. During the Christmas of 1915 we were in the front line, and it was very cold. We had our Christmas dinner there, which consisted of our regular rations, but when we came to our billets again, after six days in the front line, we had a Christmas dinner which consisted of turkey, dressing, pudding, tea, and other nice things. I am sure all the boys enjoyed it to their heart's content. In fact, it was the best meal we had since arriving in Flanders. We also had our New Year's dinner out on the line, much to our joy. During Christmas and New Year's we had entertainments at the Y. M. C. A. huts and a few movie shows.

About two days after New Year's we went back into the line; also the mud and water. The rest of that winter was very uneventful.

It was on June 21, 1916, that the third battle of Ypres started, our regiment being in the line at Kemmel Hill, and our 3rd Canadian division at Ypres. On the second of that month "Fritzie" made his drive for Ypres. The battle started about 2 A.M. The Huns came over in massed formation, and very strong in number, almost six to one of "ours." All the boys in my battalion were sitting on top of the trench, looking on at the attack. The noise from the big guns was dreadful; also the machine gun fire. The prettiest sight I ever saw was the star shells bursting in the air. They were of colored red, white, and green, which was the Hun's S. O. S. call.

On the fourth of June, "Fritzie" managed to drive our boys from their position in that part of the line. Our third division put up a very strong fight, but they were outnumbered and could not hold. So the Huns advanced quite a bit, and gained a lot of ground. The 48th Battalion was separated from the other battalions and other regiments were in the same fix. That was the reason the Huns drove them back.

On the 11th of June our battalion, the 26th, was taken out of the line at Kemmel Hill, and after a few hours rest, started for the support line at Ypres, which was Bedford Farm. On arriving there we stayed for two days, and on the 12th of the next month our famous Canadian Scottish made an attack on "Fritzie" and succeeded in driving him back, after very hard fighting and hand-to-hand work.

It was on the 14th that our battalion, accompanied by others, moved up to relieve the tired-out Scotties, who were tattered and torn. They came straggling back, but not in the same strength as when they went into the conflict. They had a great number killed, wounded, and missing. As our battalion moved up the road leading to the trenches, under heavy shell fire, we lost two hundred men, killed and wounded. As we moved along, we could see our chums falling. That made us more eager to get at the Hun. On arriving in the front line, late that evening I was detailed off as a battalion runner, and, of course, it was very interesting work. I was to report at battalion headquarters which was about three-quarters of a mile behind the line. After great difficulty I found myself at that point, and reported myself to the sergeant-major. A short time after I was ordered to take a battalion into the trenches at Hooge, and after great difficulty, going over the shell-torn ground, I landed the regiment safe at their port.

On the following morning at 9 A.M. I received another order to take a dispatch to every boy in my battalion. Of course there is always two men who go with the dispatch. The idea of that is in case one man gets wounded, the other can look after his wounds, and carry on with his orders. My partner and I started out from battalion headquarters, and going up the communication trench, found it all blown to pieces, so we decided to take to the open. On arriving at a company we delivered the dispatch and went on to the next company. It was very uneventful but it took us from 9 A.M. one day until 4 A.M. the following morning to get back. On our way back we arrived at a company in time to get a little party out to headquarters, but at the same time "Fritzie" started shelling us very heavily, so we took different routes. About fifty yards from the front line my pal got a bullet in the back, which brought him down. I dressed his wound, then carried him for a distance of about fifty or sixty yards. I then laid him down, so I could get a rest and straighten myself up, but when I picked him up again he was dead. I continued the rest of my journey alone, but before long I got hit myself in both legs. I dressed them and crawled to headquarters, delivered the dispatch, then fell into a fainting spell. When I came to I found myself in a hospital in Boulogne.

Canada's casualties in the war up to eleven days before the capture of Mons on the final morning of the conflict totalled 211,358 men.

These classified as follows:
Killed in action	34,877
Died of wounds	15,457
Wounded and presumed dead	52,779
Missing in action and known prisoners of war	8,245

Canada's losses have been very great and she has fought very bravely for a just cause, the freedom of the world and everlasting peace.

WITH THE AMMUNITION TRAIN

By Frederick Gerald McAvity, Gunner No. 91805, 8th Battery, Canadian Field Artillery

IT WAS back in 1914 when the word came to Canada for soldiers to serve for King and Country. As I was very young, not quite eighteen years of age, I thought I would like to enlist, and go to war, not really knowing what I was going into.

At that time, anyone enlisting under age had to have his parents' consent, which, I will say, was no easy matter. After having a little battle of my own, with all my relatives, I finally managed to get the signature of my parents.

We went to camp a few days later and had about two months' training at Valcartier, and then sailed for England. After training a few months in the Old Country we sailed for France the early part of February, 1915, where we first got our taste of war. I was more than surprised, because I was young, and my idea of war was sniping at each other from behind a tree or stump, but this trench warfare was a new thing. At that time I was attached to an ammunition column which fed the guns with its ammunition. Then it was a case of starving the guns, because the shortage of ammunition would only allow each gun of each battalion four rounds a day and as the soldiers call it out there, they had our "wind up" all the time.

We had lost quite a number of men at Ypres and pulled out of that position for another part of the line, when I was wounded on the forenoon of September 21st. It was only a slight wound in the left foot. After a few months at the hospital and proving A-1 again, I was sent back to the line, and joined my unit at Ploegsteert in the fall of the same year. Now, as you know, the fighting was not so great, but the hardships were terrible through the winter. It is simply wonderful what a human being can stand. If anyone had told me before I enlisted that I could lay in mud and water for day in and day out, I think I would have called him a "liar," but I have come to the conclusion that nothing is impossible nowadays.

Some days when it was a little quiet, we would spend our time in fixing up our bivouac, which we had built on the ground, as huts to live in. After the winter of 1915 and the spring of 1916, we moved to the Ypres salient and we had a pretty tough time of it there, as they had us pinned in the shape of a horseshoe, and they could hit us from all sides except the rear. The Germans had us overwhelmed at that time, but even with their wonderful fighting mechanism, they couldn't drive back the fighting race from North America.

We fought on in the salient until July, 1916, when the first division got word we were to move to another front. It was rather a surprise. We thought we were to have a rest at that time. The fighting was heavy on the two fronts—the Somme front in France and the Salonica front in Greece. So it was a question with the boys which one we were going to. At last word came to move somewhere and after a number of days on the train and on foot, we at last came to a sign along the roadway marked Somme River.

Well, then we knew we were on our way to the Somme front, going into action the same night. We arrived on the battle scene, and that was the introduction of the Canadians in the Battle of the Somme. It was a tough fight and we lost a number of men, but it was much worse for poor "Fritzie."

We had it pretty rough all the time on the Somme, and oftentimes when the rations did not get up from the divisional train, we had to lay back on the hard-tack, which looks like dog biscuits, and we thought one of these biscuits dipped in bacon grease was a great treat at that time.

I fought on the Somme through the summer of 1916, until the fall of the same year, and in the early part of the evening of November 9, as I was in horse lines of our battery, having a nice friendly game of "crown and anchor," the corporal of my section called me from my game (I was winning and did not like to leave the game) and said:

"McAvity, you will go up with rations to the battalion tonight. I think you had better leave about eight o'clock." Well, I went back to the game and played until eight, and then I started for the line. As we placed the rations over pack horses and started to plow through the mud, leading our horses, it was a case of ups and downs, stepping in a shell-hole here, and on a dead body there. Fritz was putting a lot of gas shells over, and it was getting late in the night and raining like Hell.

We had one of our boys up in the air by the concussion of a shell and he also lost his ration. At last we got to the battery. The gas shells still poured over and the major gave us orders to get back as quickly as possible after delivering the goods. I think we were about fifty yards away from the battery when a big shell burst, or at least a "Jack Johnson" as the boys call it. The boy behind me, the one who lost his ration, said to me:

"Mac, we had better hurry as it was pretty close," and let me tell you the next one that came over "got" both of us, killing him and wounding me severely. At 11.20 P.M. on the eve of November 9th, after spending nearly two years in hospital, I was discharged, May, 1918, in St. John, N. B., Canada.

HOSPITAL EXPERIENCE

By Gunner Frederick Gerald McAvity

BEING wounded on November 9th, my first stop was at a stationary hospital, Rouen, France. I had one operation there, and had some shrapnel removed from my body. One of the pieces was taken from my left shoulder; a nice-sized piece. When I came to, after being under the operation, I felt something hard on my shoulder. The nurse, seeing that I did not pay much attention to it, came to my bed and asked me if I did not want my souvenir, meaning my shrapnel. Well, as I was in great pain at that time, I did not prize it very much, but I value it quite a lot today.

After a few months in France, they moved me to a Red Cross hospital at Southampton, England, called Netley hospital. I had a long stretch of hospital life in Netley. When I was sailing from France to England, aboard the hospital ship, they asked me where I would like to go. Naturally, being a Canadian, and having no relatives over there, I promptly said, London, so I could meet some of my pals. When I got off the boat, and aboard the hospital train, I asked the orderly if I was near London, and he gave the answer: "Don't worry. You are not going to London. You are on your way to Netley, and will be there in ten minutes."

I was a little downhearted at first, but after a few weeks, I was satisfied with my treatment, which was the very best.

When I got my little lot of wounds, on the Somme, I also was exposed to gas shells, which left my stomach in such a condition that I could not eat for two months until after I had that sea voyage from France to Netley. The nurse there asked me if I would try a poached egg on toast, and that was my turning point. From that day until the day I was discharged I have not missed a meal, except after an operation.

I had nine operations altogether, eight in the Netley Hospital at Southampton, England. After the shrapnel was removed, the doctor found out that the bone in my shoulder was severely fractured, and I had four different operations, just to clean out the loose bone which was keeping my wound from healing. All the time I was in the hospital and even until three months ago my arm was completely paralyzed. But through the wonderful treatment they gave me I am very glad to say I have pretty good use of my left arm.

Another one of my large wounds was in my left thigh, where I lost about eight inches of flesh, from the knee up. I have had four operations on this limb. I lay for eight months in suspense, awaiting the official word, whether I would have to lose the left limb. I can honestly say I had a great deal of confidence in my surgeon, and one day he came to me and had a personal chat with me. He talked to me just like a father. He asked me if I thought I could stand another operation because he stated that I was in a pretty bad condition. I was very anxious to know his view on the subject, as I put all confidence in him. I promptly asked him his decision, and he replied that he thought I could stand it.

Knowing he thought I could pull through, it did not take me long to let him do anything to get me healed up.

The operation was performed and I had all the skin taken from my right thigh and grafted on the wound on the left. I can say it was a success, and after a few months I was able to get along on a cane. The doctor, seeing I was able to move about, had me sent to a Canadian Hospital so I could be boarded and sent to Canada.

I was in the Canadian hospital for about a month and was very anxious to see my native land again, when one day at noon the word came for me to pack up and get ready for the boat.

After nine days at sea on a hospital ship, with all lights aglow, at the time the Germans were sinking Red Cross ships, we pulled into Halifax, N. S., safe and sound. Here I was detailed off for a hospital, after I had my furlough, to visit my relatives.

After I had seen my people, and was exhausted from talking, and shaking hands with old acquaintances, I reported to hospital again in St. John, N. B., Canada, where I received electrical and massage treatment.

At that time I could not bend my knee, and my leg was stiff, but through the wonderful treatment, and my own will power, I finally got very good use of it before I got my discharge, May, 1918.

BUCKINGHAM PALACE
5th October, 1915.
It is a matter of sincere regret to me that the death of Colour-Sergeant Frederick William Hall deprived me of the pride of personally conferring upon him the Victoria Cross, the greatest of all Military Distinctions.

George R. I.

Mrs. M. Hall,
179 Spence Street,
Winnipeg, Canada.

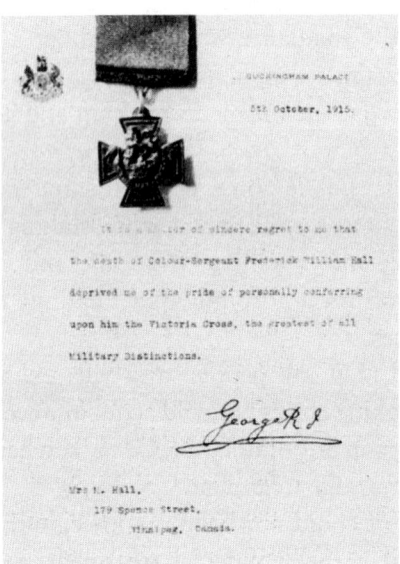

The original letter of the above photo was sent to Mrs. Hall, together with the Victoria Cross, from King George. This medal, the first Canadian Victoria Cross awarded in this War, was won by Sergeant Major F. W. Hall at Ypres, April 24, 1915, who was shortly afterwards killed in another attempt to bring in a wounded man under rifle and machine gun. The story of his two brothers appears in this book.

TWO YEARS AND A HALF OF WAR

By Sgt. F. R. Muir, No. 81611, 10th Batt., C.E.F.

SIX months before war had been declared I left New York City for Winnipeg, Canada, to play at the Winnipeg Theater and remained there until war was an established fact. On August 6, 1914, I enlisted as an American and joined the 32nd Battalion, C.E.F. After about five months' training, my battalion was ready and eager for service. From Halifax, Nova Scotia, we set out on the former Red-Star liner *Vaderland* bound for the battle grounds of Civilization, each and every boy of us keyed up to the highest pitch of patriotism. When we were three days at sea we ran out of cigarettes. A number of the boys had boxes of strong cigars with them and these they passed around quite generously. We smoked with the usual gusto and also the usual results. A ton of fish must have been fattened on food that was intended solely to strengthen us for the combat.

This experience, coupled with seasickness, made four of us refuse to wake up one morning, for which we were brought up before the major and sentenced to cleaning port-hole windows. We did not relish this labor and one port hole each was the extent of our efforts for half the day.

In the afternoon we were set to peeling potatoes, cleaning the dishes and scrubbing the lower decks, which we finally accomplished after much pouting and grumbling.

As we neared the coast of Ireland the ships which comprised our convoy seemed to be making a beeline for any port they could reach. Word had been received that subs were in the vicinity and full steam ahead was the order of the day. The fact that our ship was the slowest tub of the bunch, making only about nine knots per hour, added darned little to our comfort. Finally after much excitement we docked at Queenstown. Major Ashton, in command of our battalion, had the gangplanks lowered and invited us out to a route march through the city. We aroused quite some enthusiasm and curiosity, as we were the first Canadian troops to ever land in Ireland. Our next stop was Liverpool and there the dinkey trains, which to us were a real joke in comparison to our own huge monsters at home, afforded us opportunity for funny comment. These trains are little bits of things and from fifteen to twenty men were crammed into a small compartment normally holding about ten. Several of us were unable to sit down all the way to London. The best feature of the train service was the fond good-byes, given us by the young ladies who usually gave them with a kiss, something that not many of us found fault with.

On our journey through London we were royally received by English Red Cross ladies who fed us with welcome lunches that sure did fill the vacuum beneath the belt. From Folkestone, fully equipped, we left for France. We knew we were going over to reinforce the gallant 10th Battalion, and this knowledge added to our good spirits. We were relieving real heroes and we knew it was up to us to "Carry on" as nobly as had our predecessors. Every mother's son of us was eager, yes, anxious, to start in on real action. Canada expected much from us, and we would not disappoint her. Arriving at Boulogne we were a bit peeved as we anticipated being received by enemy shell fire, but silence was the only reception we got.

Red Cross ambulances were arriving in countless numbers, bringing in the wounded, and this was our first glimpse of battle's havoc. This sort of took the heart out of us, but only for a few moments, for, with that scene, came a gritting of the teeth, and on each face could be seen a newborn determination to see this thing through to a successful conclusion.

After a night spent, tentless, in the pouring rain, covered only with straw and the mean, wet sky, we entrained for an unknown destination, and landed at Poppraine, which surely looked like an unknown destination, as it was a typical jerk-water village inhabited only by a few old men and women. Through this village we hiked and up a road leading to the front line trenches. This road had been shot full of shell-holes, which made walking very uncomfortable. The further on we walked, the nearer came "Fritzie's" forty-two centimeter shells, fired from the largest cannon ever known up to that time; the "Jack Johnsons" as they were called. We were kept busy dodging the shells that seemed to burst all around us, yet never hit us, but in our hearts and souls we realized that at last we were on speaking terms with Mr. Death himself; and this sobered us up some, you bet. 'Twas no unusual thing to feel your hair stand right up straight on end and hear your knees beat a tattoo as they knocked against each other. However, we soon overcame this feeling as the purpose of our mission dawned upon us. I had a good opportunity to observe how young fellows act when each knows that death may be his portion at any moment.

In a section composed of eight men I noticed that one was laughing as lightly as though he was safe and secure at home. Another was singing a crazy song and kept marching along defying death, or any other horror, that might overtake him. Still another took the matter so seriously as to walk along in a sort of semi-conscious daze, with a look of stupidity on his face, oblivious to all surroundings. There is the case of Private Fred Wheelhouse, a Canadian lad of about twenty-two years, who while walking under fire of the German guns kept on playing his mouth organ or harmonica until struck on the head by a piece of shrapnel which killed him instantly and spattered his brains upon his nearby comrades.

This was our first casualty and right then and there we solemnly swore that we would avenge him. On April 21, 1915, while awaiting orders in our reserve trenches two miles from the front line which was being held by the Canadian troops from the 1st, 2nd, 5th, and 8th battalions, the Germans let loose a heavy gas attack upon them. At that time the gas mask was hardly known, the men being equipped with small, inefficient respirators, and naturally the casualties were very heavy. As a result the men had to fall back, losing a lot of the lighter guns. This made necessary the use of the men in the reserve trenches, and an order was immediately issued that we "stand to" ready to take our places in a counter-attack which was to be launched in the morning.

Imagine, if you can, the feelings of the lads awaiting the rising of the sun which, probably, meant the last sunrise many of them would behold. The tortures of the death-house, I am sure, are mild when compared to those endured by the boys, in the tense hours prior to the attack; especially when one has to listen to the moaning of the wounded who are being carried back of the lines. It is far from encouraging, and it did not surprise me when, after going through a night like this, that each and every one of us became fatalists. At five-thirty in the morning, the time set for the attack, we received word to go, and, believe me, we were glad of it. I felt as though I was ready for death to end my anxiety, or else to fight it out, right on the spot, to a finish. Our officer, Lieutenant Ball, was the first to jump to the front. After a lusty "Come on, boys," he shot forward into the turmoil, caused by our heavy artillery, with a recklessness bordering on insanity. His action was an inspiring one and we boys were ready to follow him to Hell, if needs be.

In that charge I enjoyed the experience of getting my first German. I crashed into him, a big burly six-footer, and now that my wish to meet one had been gratified, and I stood before him, I did not know whether to shoot him, punch him, kick him, or stick him as you would a pig. Not having much experience with the bayonet, I acted on impulse and rammed it right through his stomach. Oh, boy! What a squeal he let out. Putting my foot on his breast I pulled the bayonet from out his vitals, taking along with it his bowels. This nerved me, and I rushed forward like a raving maniac stopping for nothing. I plowed my way through them using first my butt and then the bayonet until I had rushed right into their second line, and, Holy Jerusalem!! right smack into a whole nest of them. We were proceeding rather methodically, in cleaning them out, when a shell from a "Jack Johnson" burst in the midst of our gallant little company, killing five outright and separating two from their legs and arms, I myself losing a leg and having my shoulder put out of commission. I was conscious all the time of what had happened, and managed to crawl into a shell-hole, and slap a bandage about my leg. With my shoulder I could do nothing and after lying exposed for two hours the company stretcher bearers picked me up, and carried me back to the dressing station. From there I was sent to No. 13 general hospital, Boulogne, but by the time I arrived, gangrene had set in, and the doctors there could do nothing for me. Again I was transferred, this time to London, and from there to Cambridge. A Doctor Cook, holding the rank of major, and from New York, announced he would cure me in two months. But the job was a more difficult one than he anticipated and six months was required ere I could walk again. During that time the leg had to be amputated to the knee. I was then discharged and received, from the Canadian Government, an artificial limb which I later discarded for a better one made in little old New York.

FROM ENGLAND TO FRANCE AND BACK

*By Pvt. George Oxton,
No. 81680, 10th Batt., C.E.F.*

IT WAS the latter end of the month of April, 1915, that the 32nd Canadian Battalion received orders to embark from the port of Folkestone, on the south coast of England, for the western front.

By reason of the fact that the Canadians had suffered great losses at the first battle of Ypres, our order to leave England came at an hour's notice, but the regiment to a man was extremely anxious to get over, and get busy.

While we were on board, our time was occupied by assembling our new issue of Webb Equipment, which we had practically thrown at us, prior to leaving our huts at Risborough Barracks, Shorncliffe. Consequently some of us found we were short a portion of the accoutrement while others had parts to spare. Being sociable, we were all able to make a complete rigout.

The night was of the pitch-black sort, but, thanks to the science of navigation, and sea and air escort, we docked at Boulogne, France, safe and sound, but in a drizzly rain.

As long as I live, I'll never forget the peculiar odor that filled the air while marching up the long, steep, winding road that led from the docks to the camp. It seemed miles, and more miles, long, but thank goodness, we arrived at last, to spend our first night on damp ground, or I had better say cold mud. It's very true we had canvas over us, but I'm sure the tents had just been thrown up, for it was quite as dry outside as inside.

I had no sooner put my head on my knapsack when that poor miserable little bugler bellowed out his early morning song.

On April the 27th we entrained for parts unknown, at least we poor privates didn't know where we were bound for; probably our company commander knew, and, if he was in the humor, the sergeant-major might have known also.

After traveling all night and part of the next day, packed in cattle cars like the proverbial sardines, we arrived at Poperinghe. The name was the largest portion of the town that the German gunners saw fit to leave. Detraining here, we made a rapid march to within a mile of Ypres. Here we joined our respective regiments. I went to the 10th Battalion. It had then earned the name of the "Fighting Tenth."

This night we dug ourselves in, along two sides of a large field. Each man dug a shallow hole large enough to lie down comfortably in. Owing to my height I had to dig one at least six feet in length. I was wishing, at that particular time, that I happened to be that poor miserable little bugler, as he was a little more than five feet tall.

The next morning I, for one, was up before reveille. I found it much more comfortable walking round in the cool of the morning than lying in a mud hole with only a greatcoat within a mile of me. I imagine something always happened to those lovely army blankets, for they were generally conspicuous by their absence.

The evening of the 28th was reasonably fine when we answered roll call prior to going up the line. Here we found ourselves in the last line of reserves, the idea being to get used to the "heavies." At times the shells became far too familiar with us, consequently I lost some of my best pals. We spent a week like this on the Yser Canal bank, living like the old cave dwellers, only we were not there long enough, and it wasn't peaceful enough, to construct any labyrinths. Our work consisted of making shelters, after a "Jack Johnson" had obliterated them.

On the move again, this time to billets about seven miles south of Baieulle, it took a full night to march the distance, with full kit. The roads didn't appear to get any softer, as time went by, but still one heard the everlasting (Kipling's) boots, boots, boots. As we had ten minutes each hour to rest, I was absolutely unconscious for nine and a half minutes of that time.

On the nineteenth of May, we were on foot again. I had a feeling it would not be to the last line of reserves this time. Neither it was, for, by the next night, we were heading for the front line trenches, one mile east of the village of Festubert. At dusk we traversed communication trenches to our destination: the front line on the edge of No Man's Land. At last! After training and waiting for over seven months. We relieved the Berkshires and took up our posts along with the "Little Black Devils," as the 8th Battalion is called, in a trench which was only captured from the Germans the previous day. The portion of the trench we held was dug in a roadway, and being fairly high ground was comparatively dry. This speaks wonders for a trench, for we plodded through much mud and water to reach it. Every second man was detailed to mount guard, while the remainder fought for forty winks, then relieved guard. The first two nights were uneventful, though a heavy artillery duel was the standing program.

The third night, the twenty-first, we were not going to give "Fritzie" a chance to come across, but we were going to push him back. If a man tells you he was not nervous going "Over the Top" for the first time, he lies. I felt nervous, though I never confessed it, and I wager everyone else felt the same way, as we had to wait about two hours, after being told we were going over. At eight o'clock we were sent up to a small communication trench about halfway across No Man's Land, on the side toward the enemy. It cut across diagonally. There was a good-sized gap, on which some snipers had their rifles trained. At this point, we lost a few of our company. It was a case of running the gauntlet for each man who passed it. All of us had to pass it three different times; for, in our first advance, the order was cancelled, so we had to return till later on.

About nine o'clock, at dusk, we finally went ahead to the end of the communication trench. Here we branched out on either side, and spread out in open order, to charge. By this time my nervousness had disappeared. My mind was set on the one object of getting someone—and I gripped my gun, and prayed for all the strength I could muster. With a wild cry of *"Lusitania,"* we received the orders to go. All I could do was yell to the boys to give them "beans," for I was knocked down, and found my right leg was half blown off, just below the thigh. If the boys hadn't taken their objective that night, I should have been a prisoner, instead of a hospital case, for over twenty months, in England.

> I'm just a plain buck private,
>   Who fought with Canada's Sons,
> In a regiment of the Maple Leaf,
>   That made it hot for the Huns.
>
> I'm just a plain buck private,
>   And fought on the side of right,
> To serve the world for democracy,
>   And beat the Hunnish might.
>
> I'm just a plain buck private,
>   From the land of ice and snow,
> And gave all I could, for my country,
>   To help to vanquish the Foe.

It was probably an hour or two after the advance that some of the men came to see what they could do for us. In my particular case the shrapnel, which had penetrated and completely shattered the right femur, had also numbed the nerves, therefore I was left conscious.

However, one of our battalion sergeants tied up the top of the leg for me with a length of cord, which I was always in the habit of carrying.

Four of the machine gunners, who had just returned from the new trench, made an attempt to carry me into the old communication trench, but their good intentions were completely frustrated by the company captain, a real cantankerous sort, who levelled his revolver at me, and declared he would shoot, if the boys took me in. Though I felt sore, in more ways than one, I came to the conclusion that he was perfectly right, as it might have blocked the trench to the reserves coming up.

The only thing to do was to put me on the ground again. Here I was expecting another shell every minute, but Providence evidently thought I had received my share, as I was free from any more shells, though they were bursting close at hand continually.

About 2 A.M. our battalion stretcher-bearers managed to reach the position where many more, with myself, were lying. The shelling had then subsided to a great extent, making it possible to continue the work of carrying out the wounded.

I knew one of the three men who came alongside of me with a perfectly good-looking stretcher. Though the way was long and very rocky, we finally arrived at the first aid dressing station. After resting here for probably an hour, I was conveyed in one of the "London Scottish" ambulances about five miles to a field hospital. I saw many of the boys here. Most of them appeared to be walking cases. The next thing I knew, I was placed on the operating table, where I smelled ether for the first time. I remember the doctor saying: "Be perfectly still, now, and breathe naturally." After that I knew no more till the job of inserting numerous rubber tubes through the leg was finished. Having to spend two nights on ambulances and trains, I arrived at a British base hospital in Boulogne. I remember the people cheering as our train pulled in, but I wasn't in the mood for caring what they did.

The treatment was of the best in this hospital, though I only remained in it fourteen days. In the bed next to mine there was a Scotchman who kept yelling continually. His leg had been amputated so I couldn't see what he had to kick about. Nevertheless, it made it quite impossible to get any rest at all.

On the morning of June 3rd, the doctor marked me "out," which meant that I was going to "Blighty." I hardly realized what it meant then.

Again I was on the table—this time to cut an abscess and to put a cumbersome iron splint on me. I think they called it a Hodgson's splint, one of those affairs that extended down two sides of the body to the feet. It took up a lot of room—so much so that I had to have a Ford ambulance all to myself; consequently at the boat's side I was taken for an officer and treated as one. This I didn't object to in the least.

The *Abert* set sail soon after, and about two hours afterward we were in Dover, where we entrained, in a regular hospital train. I was marked for Norwich, in the County of Norfolk, a short distance from the east coast. The night of June 5th our train pulled into Norwich station, where the Red Cross ambulance conveyed us to our hospital. I found myself in a military ward of the General Hospital of Norwich, but only for a few minutes. They discovered that the beds were too small for both myself and the splint, so I was shifted to another ward, where I was put to bed, and became very much attached to this same bed for ten long months, undergoing nine more operations in the hope of saving the limb. They eventually took it off, but I always have the consolation of knowing that I am far better off than a good many others.

Editor's Note:—The verses embodied in this story are in no way changed, but are printed exactly as Mr. Oxton delivered them to me.

H. L. F

"WHY I HATE A GERMAN"

*By Pvt. John T. Miller, No. 122957,
96th Co., 6th Regt., U. S. Marines*

ON THE afternoon of July 24, 1917, as I was walking along the streets of Detroit, Michigan, my attention was attracted by the beat of drums and the tramp of marching men. It then dawned on me that I was big enough to do my bit, so I went to the Marine recruiting office, enlisted, and was sent to Paris Island, S. C., where I was trained for four months. On January 19, 1918, I left New York and after thirteen days arrived at a port in France. It was there I got my first glimpse of war. We were loaded in box cars about half the size of American cars. They are built for eight horses, but forty marines had to spend sixty hours in them. We were then in the zone of advance, but stayed only about three weeks. We went into the line the first night. It was an experience I shall never forget. Cigarettes were barred and no loud talking permitted. I thought it very funny, but soon learned different. The third night in, "Heinie" paid us a visit. There were thirty-seven of us, holding about 500 yards of front line. This at one time was a quiet sector but it woke up on this night. We had no reserves, and retreat was impossible, so all we had to do was to stay and entertain our visitors.

There were about 250, and none of them looked starved to death. After the barrage lifted we saw some of the boys that we had traveled over three thousand miles to see. I was in a daze when I saw my first "Heinie," and he looked about as big as the Woolworth Building. But I woke up in time to realize that I had a rifle and hadn't forgotten how to use it. "Heinie" stopped in our wire and stayed there. Our visitors were all given a royal reception. Six of our boys went to the hospital but we left over a hundred of the Kaiser's boys in front of, and in, the trench, and had the trouble of burying them. From that night on we took more precaution and I was one that was made the goat. My "bunkie" and I took up our post in No Man's Land at sunset each night and stayed until midnight. We were put there for the purpose of announcing "Heinie" if he should call again.

"Heinie" did not worry me so much, but the rats, which we called "war babies," insisted on sleeping in my arms. And as we were in a position where the slightest noise would send us to the hospital or perhaps "west," the "war babies" had everything their own way. And the "cooties" would keep us company every night. They would parade up and down my back and of course I had to stand for it. I laid out there three nights with my pal. On the fourth day about five o'clock we decided to wash, as it would be the first time in five days. We got down to the spring without being seen and were enjoying a wonderful bath when the "Heinie" spotted us and started to snipe with his six-inch shells. Bill and I made for the dugout and had about two hundred feet to go when a shell hit under Bill's feet. I did not stop, for it was useless, as all I could see was blood and a part of a shattered leg. We picked Bill up in a box. It sure hit me hard, but it is all in the game. I swore that night I would get even, and I think I have. After three months in the front line, in and around Verdun, we went out for a rest, but not for long. We had been in a rest camp about ten days, when on the night of May 28th, at nine o'clock, we were ordered to move up the line, and stop "Heinie," who wanted to make Paris his headquarters. We were loaded in motor lorries and rode all night and part of the day.

We arrived at a little town and got something to eat, the first we had in twenty-four hours. We then started on a march which lasted thirty-six hours, when we arrived at a town about five miles behind the line, tired and hungry. I will go on record, right here, to say that I have been over every inch of France, in box cars, hospital trains, motor lorries, and the rest I hiked. We arrived at this town about 2 A.M. and were ordered into the line, but thanks to our commanding officer we did not go. The inhabitants had evacuated and we were told to go and sleep in any house we could find. It was here that I saw the first example of German "Kultur." In a room in the house I went into, I saw a mother with part of her head blown off, with a six-months'-old baby in her arms, both lying on the bed, dead. In the corner was a six-year-old boy who had evidently been killed by the same shell that killed the mother and baby. But with all that I had a good night's sleep, which I needed. In the morning we killed what live stock we could find, and sure did eat. That night we were ordered into the line and there we began to see real war.

"Heinie" started to send over everything he had, in the way of shells, high explosives, shrapnel, and machine gun bullets. There were no trenches and the only protection we had were the holes which we dug to lie in. Things were flying and I did not take time to get my shovel, which I had in my pack, but used my mess gear instead. We laid in those holes for three days and dared not stick our heads up. If we did it meant "taps," and that we would not have to answer "reveille" in the morning. What we had to eat we had at night, and it was very little, a French ration, consisting of "monkey meat" and French bread; but anything tasted good. One night a lad from Texas, who was not satisfied with his "Boudoir" in the ground, decided to change hotels. About that time "Heinie" saved him the trouble by sending an eight-inch H. E. which made a hole big enough to put a regiment in. So "Tex" decided to take up quarters in it. He had just arrived in his new home (or hole) when "Heinie" duplicated the order, which hit on the edge of the first hole. "Tex" came sailing over my head. I first thought he had joined the aviation, and was going to Heaven, but when I looked around there was "Tex" sitting on the ground trying to find out if he was all together, and cursing "Heinie" for being so attentive. Looking at me he said:

"Can you imagine those Dutchmen sniping at me with an eight-inch gun?"

On the afternoon of June 6th, we received orders to pack up and we all had the idea that we were to get a rest. All were counting on the sleep and bath we would have. But no such luck. It was here when the French had retreated so far that the artillery was no good to us, and the general in charge of the division said the words that will remain in history forever, "Retreat, Hell, we are going ahead." And we were ordered to go "Over the Top" at 5.15. The order came at five o'clock. I cannot describe the feeling one has while waiting for the word. It seemed to me that the time would never come. But suddenly the silence was broken by the blast of a whistle and we were on our way. The sun was shining and the country looked wonderful, and across the wheat we started, to reach our objective, which was the town of Bourches. We had gone no more than about one hundred feet when our captain, the first man to go down, was hit six times in the body. I began to realize then what we were up against, for "Heinie" must have had a million machine guns and they were all working.

The boys started to fall and all that was heard was, "I'm hit," or "Heinie got me." A lad beside me "got it" in the ankle, and said to me: "Kid, what do you think of that dirty bunch of Dutchmen? They won't even let me get started. When you get into the town, kill ten for me."

I promised him I would, and left him. I don't know whether I fulfilled my promise, but I told him I did when I saw him later in the hospital. When I arrived at the town, which was our objective, there were forty-seven left of 256 in our original company. The Germans were in one end of the town and we were in the other, and, as the reader will understand, one town could not hold both parties, so we started to move "Heinie." Some of us were detailed to put "Heinie" out and it was no easy job, for every "Heinie" had a machine gun. But it was the same old story, they would fire their guns until we were on top of them, then throw up their hands, shout "Kamerad," and beg for mercy. But after you go through as far as that, you cease to be human and don't know what mercy is. We reached our objective at

5.30 P.M. and at nine o'clock by direction of one lieutenant, the only officer left in the company, and a pal to all the boys, we had "Heinie" on the outside, the town fortified, and nine hundred men put into the position. Again, and up until the time I was hit, it was little or no sleep, for "Heinie" insisted upon coming back into the town.

On the afternoon of June 10th, I was going after some water, and some "Heinie" with a machine gun gave me my fare to the hospital, in the form of a bullet in the knee. Some of the boys carried me into a dugout, where I had to wait until dark, and then was carried to the rear, put in a Ford ambulance, and started to Paris. Twenty-seven miles in a Ford, on a stretcher, is no joy ride, but it was good enough. Then I reached the hospital in Paris. I had not had my clothes off for fifty-seven days. When I got a bath and saw a bed, with white linen and blankets, and something real to eat, I thought I was in paradise. After the operation, all I could do was to sing, "Please go away and let me sleep." After three months in the hospitals of France, I was put on a transport and started for New York. I am now in the hospital, awaiting discharge, and think it all a dream, and am in fear that some one will pinch me, and I will wake up.

"MY DUTY TO MY COUNTRY"

*By Pvt. Jack Kneeland, No. 105,
43rd Co., 5th Regt., U. S. Marines*

WHEN the great World War was raging, and the United States were preparing for any trouble that might occur between her and the Teutonic Government, I was playing in vaudeville. April 6th we received word that our Government declared war on Germany. Immediately I decided to quit the show business and go into the service, but what branch I did not know as I was unfamiliar with the different outfits of Uncle Sam's noble army and navy. As I was walking down the street I happened to notice different recruiting officers, appealing to the men to enlist in the several outfits we have, for the sake of our folks at home, and for democracy. I happened to think of the navy as a good chance, but as I wished to be in the thick of the battles and excitement I decided it was either the army or the United States Marines. While I was trying to fix my mind on what I should do, a marine sergeant came and started talking to me and asked me what I was going to do. I told him I was ready for the worst, and that I was anxious to go across the water and do my bit. He said that the United States Marines was the place for me, a boy with the spirit Americans wanted.

Well, it did not take me long to make up my mind, and shortly I was being examined by the doctor for physical fitness. I was confident I would pass the rigid test that is given to the marines as I had never had an illness of any kind in my life. After the examination I was told I was 100 per cent perfect, and sworn in as a private in the soldiers of the sea, as we call the marines. First to fight on land and sea. Three days later I was called to depart for Paris Island, S. C., where I was to get my training. I arrived the 15th of April and was immediately sent to a quarantine station where all preparations were given, such as clothes, finger prints taken, and then I was finally sworn in once more, on the 21st day of April. After all these proceedings were over, I was sent to the maneuvering ground where the greatest task lay. We drilled from morning until late in the evening, but I did not mind it as I knew that it was for a good purpose. Digging trenches, hand grenade practice, bayonet drills, and rifle practice were our continual routine, for fully three months. I was then transferred to Marine Barracks, Philadelphia, for duty, where I was assigned to the 5th Regiment to be ready for overseas duty.

On the 21st day of August, we received word to get ready to sail. We were then given overseas equipment and boarded the transport *Henderson*. We went to New York, where we loaded supplies and stores for the trip, and started on our way to No Man's Land at midnight the 22nd. As the submarines were active at that time we were somewhat delayed in getting there. But we finally arrived without a scratch. We landed on the 7th day of September in St. Nazarre, France. There we were taken to the Rue Du Chateau, where we were assigned to barracks.

Here we received our severe training. It was drill morning, school in afternoon, drill in evening, for two and a half months. After this we were ready for anything that might be needed of us.

On the 17th of November our commander received orders to take our men to the Flanders Front, where we were to hold the southeastern corner of the Marne with the Australian Anzacs. We immediately departed and arrived there on a very rainy day.

Now comes the first real encounter the Americans took part in. The Germans sent us a rapid shell fire from their position opposite to us. We immediately sent back an intense machine gun fire. The battle raged on for seventeen hours. I received a wound in the leg and was immediately sent to base hospital where I was at once treated. We were treated fine because the French now realized that we were with them in heart and soul. I remained in hospital twenty-three days, and then was sent back to the Front, this time to join the 43rd Regt., 2nd Division, who were holding a front in Belgium on the Cambrai side. We advanced and took several little towns around Soissons and stopped at St. Quentin which was being shelled by the Austrians. We took position and immediately started offensive. We succeeded in capturing two thousand prisoners who were sent to one of the French prison camps. After this encounter we were sent to rest camps, where our clothes were replaced by new ones, and allowed to visit the neighboring towns for seventy-two hours. I, with a comrade who you will read about later, went to Paris and had a very good time.

The French people could think of nothing too good for us. After having a fine time, we reported back and occupied the second line, with the Canadians, and once more at Sartormai I was sent with a message to Major General Leonard Wood. It was a dispatch of fifty-three miles and I was to do this in an hour and ten minutes. I had a Harley Twin Six, and I started out. It was about 9.30, Paris time, when I was passing through a lonely village, a German sniper picked me off in the head. I regained consciousness and fired my Colt automatic and got my man. I succeeded in reaching my destination two minutes before time; but in an unconscious condition. I guess the good Lord was good to me and brought me to life again so that I could explain my mission. I was taken to Base Hospital No. 3, where my wound was treated with care and the lead extracted. For two weeks and a half I was practically senseless. My memory was impaired, caused by the shock of the bullet, and the intense speed I was going. In this hospital I met a German who had been captured and had been sent to the hospital to be treated for a scalp wound. He was a very well-educated boy, about nineteen years old and could speak English very well.

He told me about how, against his will, he was dragged in and made to fight for Prussianism when he always believed in democracy. It almost brought tears to my eyes to listen to his story about the people who were wishing that the Kaiser and the Teutonic power would be killed, instead of taking every young fellow against his will and making him fight. I soon recovered, bid this boy good-bye, and moved on to the second division, who were still occupying Flanders Front.

One day while wading through mud, a big shell exploded in front of us and we lost a great number of men, and I fell into the shell crater with nine other men. The crater must have been forty feet deep, with about three feet of mud at the surface. Here we did not eat for five days. We had to drink the green slime and mud so that we might not perish from thirst. Every time we wanted to sleep we would fall in this mud and wake up all caked with it. We were finally rescued by a French patrol party, and given plenty of food and nourishment to put us on our feet again. We were sent to a convalescent camp, and told to do nothing but rest. After resting for a month I was again placed in position with our snipers, with Private Al Barker as my companion. I at once took position in the limbs of a tree, so that I could notice any patrols that might pass. On our southern corner we saw a raiding party of Germans, fixing their machine guns to clean up a town called St. Forme. We immediately opened fire on these men, and succeeded in picking off a large majority of them. Suddenly my comrade received a wound in the knee and fell to the ground. I descended and, picking him up, carried him safely to our lines, receiving at the same time three bullet wounds.

We were sent to Base Hospital No. 16, where we were operated on. It seemed as though it was a year before we were well. Finally we were sent to the front at Belleau Woods. This place was approximately the turning point of the war. It is situated thirty-eight miles from Paris, and the Crown Prince's army were trying to advance through it. Here for forty-eight hours we were continually on the alert, always watching the Germans. We did not eat for forty hours.

On the 18th of July at 12.03 A.M. we received the call to arms. We were ordered to advance to the Forest of Père where a great number of Germans were operating. We traveled seven and a half miles on foot and placed ourselves on the southeastern part of Chateau-Thierry. We opened fire immediately, and this is where the bloodiest encounter of our service took place. We succeeded in starving our opponents and cut off all their ammunition. It was a big disaster to us as they outnumbered us four to one. After the British had been thrown back, the marines took the field and succeeded in annihilating the Crown Prince's army.

Of our battalion, of one thousand men, only 147 survived, and practically all of these were wounded. The Germans, seeing that they were beaten, immediately sent over their fumes of deadly mustard gas and liquid fire. I happened to be one of the unlucky ones and received a big dose of it. It fairly burned the clothes from my back, blinding me instantly, and deafened me. I was taken to Base Hospital No. 23 where I remained forty-two days. After I had recovered a little I was sent to a convalescent camp to await my departure for the good old U. S. A. On September 24th I sailed from Brest and arrived safely in Hoboken, October 3, 1918.

THE "DARDANELLES" CAMPAIGN

*By Sgt. M. L. Nicholson, No. 3736,
10th Liverpool Scottish, B.E.F.*

AT THE outbreak of the war I enlisted in the 10th Liverpool Scottish Regiment, B.E.F. It was at 2.30 P.M. on September 14, 1914, I went into the recruiting office, and offered my services. The captain looked at me and said, "I am afraid you are too young." I was then seventeen years of age. With tears in my eyes I walked out only to meet my six pals who were in kilts. One of them, "Vic" Gordon, said:

"Come back at five o'clock and try again;" so I made up my mind I would get in the army at five o'clock that day, and I was accepted, I think, because they were so busy in the office that they did not notice me. Well, I went home the day after with my knees all bare; perhaps for the first time since my childhood. My folks just roared and laughed at me, saying, "You will never make a soldier," and a lot more things that made my Scotch blood boil.

I stayed at home for three days before I was called, and then, only then did I know what being a soldier meant. The first thing was to learn how to turn and salute, then came a route march, around the country for ten miles. It was no joke with great big army boots that weighed about fifteen pounds,—it seemed that much to me. After being in the army for about four weeks, we were brought to the fields to drill. What I could not understand was, that they put cows and other animals into this big field the night before and that field was just terrible for a man to walk on, let alone lay down in. We were all wondering what we were going to do, and, I can tell you, it wasn't long before we found out. The captain came up to us and said:

"All right, boys, we are ready for some drill in this field."

You should have seen the look on some of the boys' faces. I may mention that some of them were bankers and lawyers and even millionaires' sons. I heard one man say in a typical English way: "Oh! isn't the army beastly, old man."

Of course, not being used to army life, it would make any man swear, but as the days rolled on we all got used to it. They moved us from a place called "Slop Field" in Liverpool to a place called No Man's Field in Blackpool. Every day it rained we would go on this field for extended order drill. At any rate we became used to army life in, what I thought, a very short time. It was in November, 1914, about seven o'clock when we arrived at Southampton, and were put up, for the night, in stables, with damp blankets to cover ourselves. After that night I began to suspect something. I just sat down to think that they were breaking us in for France. We were in this place till December 3rd and at twelve that night we sailed for an unknown destination. We arrived at a place called Le Havre, France. There I met with an accident. A horse kicked me in the right leg, and put me out of business for a month. That was my start to see real life. I was fixed up by the Red

Cross and sent to a battalion called the Lancashire Fusileers. We left France and arrived in London, January 10th. They gave us ten days leave, and packed us on a big liner called the *Alaunia*. We left on this liner and I did not know where I was until we arrived at Gibraltar. We were there for five hours—then set sail for Malta. We received orders not to leave the ship as we would not be there more than twelve hours, and that twelve hours seemed like twelve years. We could see all the people and shops but we could not get to them. We sailed away from Malta to an unknown destination. About one hundred miles out to sea we received orders to turn back, on account of the submarines being very active around that district, but an hour after we received that message, we had orders to proceed on our journey, and all the way we could see dead horses and boxes floating on the water. We were told later that a ship had been torpedoed a short distance in front of us. We were out three days when we sighted land, and, believe me, it was a treat, as the drill on the ship was very bad. The boys had to scrub out their bunks and the decks, and others had to keep watch all night, for the little devils in the water. Anyway, it was a great relief when we disembarked at Alexandria, Egypt. It was some place. I met people from all over the world. We were taken over to the barracks and a very funny thing happened. I was in charge of twenty-four men, and let me tell you they were all rough necks. I asked one how he liked the place and he said:

"Oh, I would like to be in the Bee Hotel, playing a game of pool." He had just time to get those words out of his mouth when a man with a big cigar in his mouth put his arm around his neck and shouted:

"Tom! my dear brother."

You should have seen how they hugged and kissed each other for about fifteen minutes. All this time the rest of the boys were trying to make out the Arabs. They were visitors, looking at us with open mouths. We had our drill on a desert and with a broiling sun on us all the time. We left Alexandria the latter end of March, 1915, and arrived at Lemnos, a Greek Island, later used as a hospital base. After we left Lemnos in a convoy of about fifteen ships we arrived at our destination, the Dardanelles. All that we could see in front of us was a great big hill. Later we found out they called it Kemara Hill. The spirit of everyone was good. We were issued 200 rounds of ammunition and carried our packs on our backs. All that I could hear from the boys was:

"We will take that hill by the morning."

Little did we know what was in store for us. Orders came to disembark, so we all helped to lower the life boats, and climbed down the rope ladders into them. I was all settled down with the rest of the boys to make a clean landing without the Turks knowing. Up came a tug boat and took about ten small boats in tow.

Just at that moment we were under fire. The big battleships opened up, and it was some bombardment. The 15-inch guns on the *Queen Elizabeth* let go with the rest. We were about twenty yards off the beach when, before my eyes, I saw my comrades fall in the water, boats capsizing, rifles in the air, and arms and legs flying around. On seeing this our tug turned toward Cape Hellos, on the right of West Beach, and every man made for the water. Some managed to get on land. You see, the Turks, mastered by German officers, put barbed wire entanglements into the water. They knew we could only land in small boats, as the water was not deep enough for a liner to get close. As the life boats turned, they got tangled in the wire and overturned. Some of the boys tried to grasp hold of the wire, but had to let go, as it cut their hands, and of course they were drowned. We lost an awful number of men before the real scrap began, and I will say it was some landing. I did not believe I could come through this bit of a scrap. When I landed I looked to see if I was all there. The Turks had trenches right up to the water's edge, and, God bless those Australians, they drove the Turks out of the first line and gave us a chance to land. I asked a chap next to me what he thought of it and how he liked it. Well, he gave me a look enough to kill me, and said, "Well, the first five years is the worst. After that I suppose we will get used to it."

I was five days on land when I began to feel the strain of not having enough food or water. Water was scarce and my mouth was all blistered, it was so hot. We were getting a little supply of water and biscuits from the ships. They came in gasoline cans that had not been washed out properly, but we were so thirsty that we did not bother about the taste.

When I received my wound on the head, I did not know what hit me, but I found myself on board a boat called *Andania*, a sister ship to the one I left England in. I had a big bandage stuck on my head and was shipped to Lemnos. I lost my memory for a bit and they called me a serious case, so they packed me to a hospital in Alexandria. I fell unconscious again for ten hours and, as I opened my eyes, I could just see a pair of lovely blue ones looking down at me, and a little motherly hand grasped mine. I cannot explain the feeling in my heart in words, when I saw it was a mother. I called her mother because she was a Red Cross nurse. The first thing she asked me was, "Can I write a letter home for you?" You can imagine what I said. I had not heard from home since I left, and I told her to write and say I was all right and would be home soon. I was in that hospital three weeks and every day I would ask that lovely mother to write for me, as I was too weak to write myself. It broke my heart when I had to leave that hospital, as all the nurses were so kind to me. I sailed on a hospital ship for England and was put in a hospital in Liverpool, my own home town. In this hospital there was a funny Irish boy who had come from France and was all covered with bandages. I made a pal of him, and the jokes he used to tell me made me forget the pain. One Wednesday a lady came to see us in the hospital and looked at me, saying:

"Were you hurt at the Front," and my Irish pal answered for me, saying: "No, ma'am, sure he tripped over a match stick and sure a fly kicked him."

Oh, he was full of the devil. On leaving that hospital I got a month's leave to recuperate, and spent it at home. I was recalled for service at the end of the month to my delight, as I wanted to see some more fighting. I was attached to the 2nd Battalion of the 10th Liverpool Scottish, and we were detailed to go to France.

"THE FIRST OF THE TANKS"

By Sergt. M. L. Nicholson

RUSHED out of the pleasant atmosphere of an English hospital into France, thence to Arras, to help extend the British front, was my next little bit of adventure. Arras at that time was a sort of resting place, as the fighting there was not half so severe as at Gallipoli, and besides it was held on a fifty-fifty basis, the Germans holding one-half the village and the British the other.

Vimy Ridge, nearby, and Arras were well sown with mines, and this being known to the enemy, we were not molested by surprise attacks as we otherwise would have been. Close upon Arras stood Devil's Wood, a point of vantage to whichever side could hold it. It was a much sought-after place and had recently been wrested from the British. It was up to the newcomers, mostly from the 1st King's Liverpool Regiment, to regain it. Needless to say we did this thoroughly and kept on advancing to Fleurs.

At this stage of the game a great surprise was sprung on us. We were keyed up to the highest point, ready for battle, and it was to be our first attack on Fleurs, when of a sudden we were drenched by a deluge of tear shells. A tear shell is one of the meanest of all shells, as it gives out a poison that causes the tear ducts to turn almost inside out and the tears, which continually flow, change to a sickly looking green fluid. On top of that, we were also treated to a breakfast of liquid gas and, believe me, I got my fill on that memorable morning.

To make sure that I was "out" for good, a stray piece of shrapnel found its way through my helmet and opened a three-inch scalp wound which I had received, as a souvenir, from a Turk at the Dardanelles. The photograph shows how my helmet suffered.

The gas attack in the morning temporarily blinded my right eye. However, all these minor affairs did not occur until after I had witnessed the greatest surprise of the war.

It was at the "Zero Hour," and we were nervously awaiting the word to go over, when five huge, lumbering monsters crept forward from our lines. Could this be a bad dream, or were we seeing things. But look! They are spitting fire! They don't stop! Down into a trench and over they go. Barbed wire is like a spider's web to them! God! how they travel, these animated blocks of steel. They look like caterpillars or frogs. They look like every living thing that crawls, and the enemy's shells fall from them like water from a duck's back. Onward they go and we are told to follow them. The rest is history. They were the first five "tanks" used in the war and, at once, were recognized as the most terrible of all engines of destruction. Their presence revived our fellows as though an electric current had passed through them. These first "tanks" were a symbol of our strength and determination to win and when we saw them sweep forward majestically, literally eating up the Hun devils, my heart was glad, and the pain of my wounds vanished. The boys now had a fighting chance against the wicked machinations of the foe. We had gone the enemy one better, at his own game of inventions, and Victory was only a question of building more "tanks" behind which the infantry could find shelter in the attack.

THE SUNSHINE OF THE TRENCHES

By Sgt. E. D. G. Aylen, No. 475337, P.P.C.L.I. ("Princess Pats") C.E.F.

I HAD just returned from a long summer's work on a surveying party, on the Canadian Pacific Railway, and everybody in my home town, Montreal (that is, the men), were all dressed in uniform, and the women seemed to be looking at me, and at first I felt uncomfortable and wondered why they stared at me. Then I realized that I had just returned from the brush of the great Canadian northwest. I knew, of course, that there was a war on, and the boys were going over, but for the moment, on my arrival in town, forgot.

The boy friends whom I chummed with were overseas, and my blood began to boil. I was then nineteen years of age, and was quite eligible for service. After a few days at home, I announced, to my mother and father, that I was going overseas. Both objected and said that I should take out a commission. That did not suit me, and I thought of the quickest way to get over.

On my way to "McGill" one morning I stopped to talk to two boys in uniform. I asked them how they liked the army and what unit they belonged to. One said:

"Army life is great. We are 'University' boys to reinforce the famous 'Princess Pats,' and I believe it is the quickest way over." That was just what I wanted, and I asked the boys to go with me to the recruiting office, which they did.

Corporal Coate was there to greet us, and it was not long before I was signed up. After all sorts of questions I was given a small slip of paper with my number on it (No. 475337) and a hat badge with "Universities Overseas Company," and on my shoulders were letters that read P.P.C.L.I. ("Princess Patricia's Canadian Light Infantry"). I had heard all about the famous "Pats" and was of course glad that I was to be one of them.

It was September 28, 1915, that I was sworn in as a soldier and I felt fine. We trained in Canada, at McGill University, for two months and had it not been for the war I would have been well on my way as a student of that university. We had guard work to do, physical training, and route marching; then word was passed around that we were to go overseas and we were all delighted, as none of us wanted to be "Home Guards."

On November the 15th, we left Montreal by train, amid the cheering crowds of our friends, sweethearts, and mothers. Two days after we arrived at Halifax, where we embarked at 5 P.M. on the *S.S. Lapland*. The people in Halifax were there to mail letters or postal cards for us, which we threw from the steamer.

At 7 P.M. we set out on our long voyage, and, as the boat steamed out, the band on the deck played "When the Roll is Called Up Yonder I'll be There," but the funny part was, that every member of the band was about sixty years old, and we knew he "wouldn't be there."

We had eight good days going over and all enjoyed it, except a few who treated the fish in the ocean.

The latter part of November we arrived in England at Plymouth, and, in the rain, embarked on a train to our training camp at St. Martin's Plain near Shorncliffe. As you know, we trained there, but that will not interest you as much as our time in France, so I will skip that to the day we sailed for France.

At 4 A.M. we all fell in and the roll call was taken. We marched to the train, after having our pay book made up to date. We never forgot the pay book or the dinner call. A thing that all the boys noticed was that we were to cross the channel from Southampton on the S.S. *Duke of Connaught*, a fitting place for "Princess Pats." Other boys said that was luck. It was for some of us. We arrived at Havre, France, and in the rain marched seven miles to a camp called the Central Training Camp, where we spent a few days receiving instructions in modern warfare.

After the few days in camp we marched seven miles back again to Havre, and proceeded by train by Poperinghe in those beautiful Pullman cars, marked 40 men—8 horses.

We arrived at Poperinghe at 5 P.M., after spending all night, and part of the next day, in the cars. As we came nearer to our station we could hear the shells bursting and the booming of the guns. One could see nothing but heads stuck out of the car windows just as far as craning necks could stretch.

Arriving at Poperinghe we met a lieutenant who asked the sergeant:

"Are you for the 'Pats'?" the sergeant replying, "Yes, sir." In a very English way the lieutenant said:

"Oh, very well, follow me. I know where the 'Pats' are, as I was sent for you."

Well, we followed him. He took us four miles the wrong way and back again—then we had an extra two miles to the "Pats" quarters. He knew where the "Pats" were all right, all right.

Now we are with the regiment and I was put in No. 3 company under Major Charlie Stewart, who was one good fellow. The regiment was out for rest, but we worked every night going up the line to do work in the trenches, and help the engineers.

Now to tell of one or two little experiences in the front line, say about the time of the "Third Battle of Ypres." The regiment held the line at Hooge and we were all University men, as the old regiment was practically all wiped out, except a handful. Our major was well liked, and a word from him was well obeyed.

A few days before the big show I was sent out on a scouting party of twelve, with Lieutenant Fife in charge. We succeeded in getting over to the German wire, and I don't know whether the Germans got wise to our coming, through the sneezing of one of the party, or whether the clipping of the wire was heard. But we were greeted with, first a rifle shot from a sniper, then a bomb; then a dozen, but only two of the boys were killed. We moved further up the line and a little closer to "Fritzie's" line. There we remained quiet for a few seconds. I, being near Lieutenant Fife, was asked by him to follow, which I did. He went up to a part of the Hun's line that was built of old sand bags, where we could look right up the German line, as the star-shell burst and lit up the place.

As everything was quiet, the boys were anxious to start something, so a few bombs were hurled in, but in return we had the same amount, and had to return to our own lines minus two of the boys.

It was on a working party that some fun occurred, as it always does in the trenches. We were moving from the road, to proceed up the "China wall," in the Ypres salient, which led to the trenches, running through the shattered village of Hooge, when the sergeant-major said to me:

"Aylen, special duty, step out."

I thought, "I wonder what is coming now."

After he had the number of men he wanted, and all the other boys were up the line, he called me and pointing to twelve large thermos soup tanks, said:

"See those, Aylen?"

I said, "Yes, sir."

"Well," he said, "take them up the line."

I looked at him and then at the tanks and said:

"Shall I take them all up at once, or one at a time?"

He gave me one look and said, "Don't get funny, this is a soft job for you."

I said, "But I can't carry those up."

He said, "You must."

Now the soup tanks were about four feet high and about a foot in diameter.

I said again, "Sir, I can't carry that up."

He, a little angry, said, "You must."

I said, "I can't carry it—it is bigger than I am."

Then he said, "Well, a man is to help you."

So he sent a man, whose name was Cleary, an Irishman,

about six feet two inches tall, and as I was only five feet five inches, it was going to be rather awkward for us both, as you have to put a long pole through the loops on each side of the tank, and put the pole on your shoulders. The tank hangs in the center. Cleary being taller than I, and the trench mats very slippery we had "one —— of a time." I was getting the worst of it. We slipped and stumbled and spoke about a hundred different kinds of "swear words." Now the "China wall" ends about halfway up, and we then stepped down into the trench. Just about twenty feet away from the end of the "China wall" there was a large shell-hole and our trench mats, which are made of wood, went across one side of the shell-hole. When the shell-hole is full of muddy water the trench mats float. This night Cleary and I happened to pass it when it was full. It was very dark and I did not notice that the mat was loose, as I was leading, so upon putting my foot on the mat, down it went. The hole was about eight feet deep, and I felt it going from under me and pulled on the pole. Soup tank, pole, and Cleary, and all followed me into that shell-hole. When we came up covered with that lovely, slimy mud, you couldn't tell which was the soup tank. Then I remembered what the sergeant-major had said, "This is a soft job for you,"—and, believe me, it was.

There is one thing I would like to say and that is the boys of the Princess Pats had wonderful courage, and always a good word for each other. I can picture plainly our trip over the top at Hooge, when I went over with the second wave. I could see the boys on our left going through a swamp up to their waists in filth; plowing through, their rifles up over their heads, so they would not get blocked with dirt, and when a man met a bullet with "his number," he would fall backward or forward and disappear under this water and mud; just like quicksand.

It was after a terrific bombardment of our lines. I was detailed to fill sand bags in a shell-hole beside a communication trench, just back of the front lines. I was with five other chums, when a shell dropped on the far corner of the shell-hole, which I was facing, and the shrapnel penetrated my left shoulder, mouth, right eye and a small piece in my left leg. My chum, Nelson, was badly wounded in the back, and I believe the other four boys were buried. I never heard if they got them out, as I was unconscious, but when I was struck I can remember, first seeing a green light, felt a burning in my eye, and a blow on my shoulder as if struck with a sledge-hammer. I felt myself slide down in the mud and I knew nothing until I awoke in the major's dugout. I was told what had happened to the other boys.

I was then taken to the dressing station and in two days arrived at No. 3 Canadian General Hospital at Boulogne.

I was blind in both eyes for a month, had two operations in France, and was then sent to England to the 4th London General Hospital, Denmark Hill. After spending a few months there I was sent to the C.C.A.C. (Canadian Casualty Assembly Centre), better known as "Charlie Chaplin's." This was at Folkestone. After having two "boards" they found me unfit for further service in England or France, so I was billed for Canada.

Arriving in Canada on the *S.S. Empress of Britain*, at Quebec, I was sent to the convalescent home (Belmont Park) at Montreal, and after treatment was honorably discharged as physically unfit.

I trained in the McGill O. T. C. and later came to New York with the "British Canadian Recruiting Mission," where I lectured, and did recruiting work, through New York City. Since leaving the mission I have traveled to the West Indies and through the eastern part of the United States. Many of my experiences I have omitted on account of space, but I am proud to have belonged to a famous regiment, "The Princess Pats."

MY EXPERIENCES IN FRANCE WITH THE 10th CANADIAN INFANTRY

By Sgt. Harry Hall, No. 19805

WHEN Great Britain declared war on Germany, I considered it my duty as a member of the Canadian Militia to volunteer my services for the Front.

The 106th Winnipeg Light Infantry to which I belonged, was the first infantry regiment to leave Western Canada to join the mobilization camp at Valcartier, Quebec.

Under the new scheme of organization, every regiment lost its identity and we were merged into the 10th Battalion, Second Infantry Brigade.

Early in October we left Canada for England, arriving at Plymouth and were then taken by train to Salisbury Plains, which is noted for mud and rain.

After undergoing training in the winter, we embarked at Avonmouth, Bristol, and sailed for France in a cattle boat, landing at St. Naize in the Bay of Biscay, four days later.

Then we had two days traveling in a box car up to the Trout, and after a short rest we went to Ploegsteert Woods and went under a system of training with the Dublin Fusileers.

The method of training we went through was excellent in every way, each one of us being posted with one of the Dublins and to do what they did.

When we reached the trenches, I was posted with "Spud Murphy" who was then on sentry go. Spud was a hero of "Mons," having had safely survived up to the present and so we had quite a lot to talk about.

Ploegsteert being a quiet "front," there was nothing very exciting, so we were pleased when we were shifted to the village of Fleurbaix to relieve an English division and to take trenches over on our own.

We were placed on the line near the village of La Boutillerie, where the trenches cut through the walls of a convent.

The Germans were about 150 yards away and seemed to have well-constructed trenches.

During the first night in, one of the Germans shouted over and asked what part of Canada we were from. How they learned that the Canadians were in front of them I have no idea, but as they had plenty of spies in our rear, they must have received the information from them.

The Germans were in happy spirits that night, as they were singing and playing instruments almost until dawn; one of them had a fine baritone voice and sang several songs in English, including "Rocked in the Cradle of the Deep." I think they were Saxons, as it was never customary for the Prussians or Bavarians to act in that manner.

Although the trenches were wet and muddy, things were not too bad, as we were allowed to build fires so we could warm our machonichie rations and also make tea.

There was hardly any artillery fire, but the German snipers

were very clever in that region and it meant death to show a head. I had one periscope shot out of my hands which will show what their snipers can do.

After three days in, we were taken out for a rest and billeted in a school house in Fleurbaix.

The next time we went to the front line, my platoon was ordered to man a redoubt behind the front trench. The idea of a redoubt is in case the enemy breaks through the front line the men manning it can pour enfilade fire into the enemy while they are passing in their advance to the second line of trenches.

This particular redoubt was a circular sandbagged construction large enough to allow sixty men to fire through the loopholes, and had two lines of entanglements round it with one narrow path through them to enable us to get in or out. This pathway could easily be blocked by a mass of wire called a "Chevaux de Frize," which was kept in the redoubt, and which could be placed in position when we had all entered.

Food which would last a platoon for ten days and a barrel of water was always kept in stock and was only allowed to be used in case the garrison was besieged. Things being quiet at this time, we had permission to use a cottage, which was only a few yards away, to sleep in at nights.

On the second day we remained in the cottage for part of the time, but as we had lit a fire to cook the dinner on, the Germans must have seen smoke coming out of the chimney, and soon got our range with one of their 77MM. field guns. The second shell hit the roof of the cottage, bursting, the shrapnel bullets were scattered in the next room to where I was.

The platoon lieutenant was in the room when the shell burst, and was talking to a sergeant and a corporal; the corporal was hit in thirty-one places down his left side, and was in a terrible mess. The lieutenant was wounded in the arm and the sergeant in the leg. The rest of us picking them up, rushed to the redoubt, another shell hitting the cottage just after we left. This taught us a lesson, and for the next few days we stayed under cover.

We were moved to the Ypres front in April to relieve a French division, marching twenty-two miles from Estaires to Abeele in one day, with full marching order, including 150 rounds of ammunition. The battalion rested at Abeele for a few days and then we marched through Poperinghe and the town of Ypres up to the front line.

At last we were in the dreaded Ypres salient, the worst sector of the front, and on which the Germans had sacrificed thousands of men in an effort to gain Ypres and the roads to the Channel ports. As the French came down one side of the road, we went up the other into the front line; at the part we were on, the trenches cut across the Polccapelle Paschendale Road, where the British Seventh Division cut the Prussian Guards to pieces the previous October.

The next morning we could see hundreds of dead Germans lying beyond our entanglements who had been dead five months, and as there was a light mist which would easily hide us, the German trenches being 800 yards away, a few of us crawled through the wire and went to have a look at them.

By their epaulettes, we could see that they were the 235th Prussian Regiment, and they must have had a terrible list of casualties by the number who were dead. Any German shell which dropped short fell among them and many had heads and legs missing; the stench was so bad that two of our men vomited, and it was a sight that no doctor would recommend for anyone suffering from shattered nerves.

After six days up there in the badly constructed trenches and under continual bombardment, without a hot drink all the time, working like slaves every night, filling sandbags and strengthening the parapets, our appetites spoiled by the sights and stench of the dead "Fritzies," we were at last relieved by our 5th Battalion, and marched into Ypres to the billets, which were in a large mill alongside the Yser Canal.

Ypres at this time was full of the civilian population and Estaminets. Restaurants and the market-place were open, so we had a splendid opportunity to change our diet from the everlasting bully and biscuits.

Two days after we entered Ypres the Germans opened up their great offensive on the 22d of April, where they used their poisonous gases for the first time. They also commenced to shell the town with every sized gun they had, from 18 pounders to their 14-inch Austrian Skoda howitzers, the largest caliber gun used on the western front.

Scores of civilians were killed as they rushed out of the town, and it was pitiful to see the little children lying dead in the streets.

The Germans broke through the Algerians on our left flank under cover of their poisonous gases, which killed thousands of Algerians and our own men in the front line trenches.

Our battalion and the 16th Canadian Scottish were the only reserves in the whole salient, and as the Germans had broken through, things were looking very black for us.

We were instantly summoned to "fall in" and soon we were on our way to fill the gap. We were two thousand men to stop the German divisions in their countless thousands.

An ordinary general would have posted us in a reserve line of trenches until the Germans advanced the next morning, but not so General Alderson, our divisional commander, an English general, who proved himself one of the geniuses of the war. He tried strategy, which was one of the biggest bluffs of the war, and which utterly surprised the Germans.

Instead of waiting for the Germans to swamp us the next morning with their greater superiority of twenty to one man, he ordered us to make a night attack on the Pilkem Woods, where the Germans were massing for their attack.

The attack was made in lines of double companies, 500 men in each of the four lines, A and B Company of our battalion being in the front line and supported by C and D Company, and then the 16th Battalion behind them.

Unsupported by artillery, we advanced shortly after midnight, getting to within thirty yards of the Germans before being discovered.

The Germans at once opened up "rapid fire" with every machine gun and rifle they had, the night air being rent with the cracks of hundreds of rifles and machine guns.

How any man could pass through that hail of lead has always been a mystery to me, but the remnants of us, after a desperate struggle in the dim light, took possession of the wood at the point of the bayonet.

The German garrison was completely demoralized, and our impetuous advance did not cease until we reached the far side of the wood, and there we entrenched.

An hour later, a most formidable concentration of artillery sweeping the wood, as a tropical storm sweeps the forest, made it impossible for us to hold the position.

Instead of retiring, we tried our old tactics of advancing, and attacked the Germans once more, who were digging themselves in about 200 yards in front.

We soon gained an objective and remained there until the next day. Our ranks by this time were sadly depleted. Our colonel was killed and only two officers still remained in the fight.

We were still losing men, owing to the German artillery fire, and our ranks being now so thin, it was inadvisable for us to remain out in that exposed position.

Fifteen hundred men had already fallen, and what could the remaining 500 of us do against the German hordes?

Sick as we were with the gas fumes and the terrific strain we had undergone, we retreated back through the wood to an old line of trenches and there waited for reinforcements.

Our object had been achieved, the Germans were demoralized, and puzzled as to how many men we had.

Their proposed attack was cancelled for a few hours to enable them to re-form and organize, and by the next hour or two our reinforcements would have arrived.

Our first brigade appeared on the scene and the line was strengthened, and then the Buffs, the famous English regiment, came up at the double after having marched miles from another part of the line.

The bluff that we pulled off was therefore entirely successful, and the Germans thought that we had about 20,000 men attacking them.

It never struck their imaginative, cold-blooded, and calculating minds that 2,000 men would have the audacity to attack whole German divisions without artillery support.

They certainly have had many lessons showing the difference between spirit and material.

The charge we made stands out as one of the finest achievements of the war, and only equaled, in the estimation of British experts, by the wonderful charge of the Worcestershire Regiment, who with only 500 men charged a division of Prussian Guards at Gheluvelt in October, 1917; also the famous Black Watch and the Scots Greys in their spectacular stirrup at St. Quentin.

It will always be a source of pleasure to me to know that I was in the front line of the first attack made by soldiers from the continent of America and was in the Battle of Ypres, which made the name of Canada ring through the world.

Remaining on Ypres front for several days, the remnants of the battalion were taken to the rear to await for reinforcements. These, in due course, arrived, and we were then sent to Festubert, and on May 17th our remade infantry brigades advanced toward the firing line once more.

On the 21st of May we went "Over the Top" at Festubert, with the object of capturing a strong German redoubt called "Bechill."

My platoon was practically annihilated by machine guns and none of us succeeded in passing the entanglements; over fifty of the men of the platoon, which numbered sixty, being killed or wounded in less than two minutes.

The rest of us, seeing that things were hopeless, retired to an old communication trench and made our way to bomb our way past the barricade which led to the redoubt.

As we threw bombs over the barricade, the Germans retaliated, and I discovered that it is impossible to indulge in the practice of throwing grenades for any length of time without someone getting hurt. At this time a German bomb fell in the bottom of our trench and burst there, wounding three of us, myself getting a piece of shell in the foot.

I was in the hospital only three weeks, and then returned to the battalion, who were on the La Bassee front.

On the third day of my second time in the trenches at Givenchy, the Germans opened up a bombardment with high explosives, and while walking up a communication trench an 8-inch German shrapnel burst in the air, and one piece of shell hit my ammunition pouches, while another passed through my arm and then hit my side.

While in the hospital, gangrene possomy set in and I was sent to Glasgow, Scotland, where I remained for many weeks.

My arm being partly paralyzed, I was returned to Canada and discharged in May, 1916.

Two weeks after I joined the Canadian Active Militia (pay corps), and was promoted to sergeant, but never recovered the full use of my arm, and consequently was unable to return to France.

THREE YEARS AND TWO MONTHS IN FRANCE

*By Lance Corporal Edmund Hall,
2nd Scottish Rifles, B.E.F.*

AFTER being in the army eleven years and with one year to go to finish my time as a regular soldier of the British Army, for which period I had signed on, I was beginning to think that I would be unfortunate enough to finish my soldiering without seeing active service, but after all I was not to be disappointed and I saw more active service than ever I bargained for.

At the time Great Britain declared war on Germany I was stationed with the British garrison at Malta, an island fortress in the Mediterranean Sea, where in peace time a garrison is kept consisting of five regiments of infantry and several batteries of artillery. On the 4th of August we received orders to proceed from barracks to take up positions in the land entrenchments and redoubts, as an attack was expected from part of the German fleet, the *Goeben* and *Breslau* at the time being somewhere in the vicinity.

The attack which we expected did not materialize, as the German ships ran for cover to the Golden Horn and Constantinople, and were afforded shelter by the Turks. In this respect they were as fortunate as their sister ships who had the protection of the Kiel Canal. We were now waiting for the territorial battalions which were to relieve us so that we could take our place on the western front and fight with the regulars who were stemming the German tide in Flanders. On the 17th of September our relief arrived, and the ships which brought them to Malta took us to England, and we were camped for a time at Winchester while our division was being mobilized. This division, the 8th, was made up of regulars from foreign service and included regiments from Gibraltar, Egypt, India, and our own from Malta. The average service of the men of the Scottish Rifles was seven years and we were in the best of training, having just finished maneuvers. It was this training, excellent shooting, and individual initiative which earned for us the praise of the Germans, who said that every British regular was a trained non-commissioned officer. We landed in France on the 5th of November, 1914, and entrained for the railhead nearest the Neuve Eglise and Massines front. This front at the time was being taken over from the French and we relieved one of their regiments in the front line of trenches. At this time of the campaign, trench warfare was just beginning, as the fighting previously at Mons, Marne, and the Aisne was a retreat or an advance and was mostly field warfare. The Germans having failed in their terrific drive for the Channel Ports during the first battle of Ypres, where the flower of the Prussian Guard had been destroyed by our 7th Division, decided to dig themselves in and to wait for the spring before opening another offensive on a large scale. Consequently, when we relieved the French the trenches were little better than ditches, and we had not even sandbagged parapets erected or barbed wire entanglements thrown out in front. It was the surprise of my life when our platoon officer informed us that the particular part of the ditch which we were in was a trench, and was to be our home for the next few days. A local attack from the Germans was expected at any time, as they were anxious to get command of the Messines Ridge, ground which they coveted for observation purposes. The French had warned us to be particularly on the lookout this night, and advised us to post extra sentries, and it was very fortunate that we heeded their warning, because about two hours after the sentries shouted from the listening posts that the Germans were coming. The company commander gave us instructions not to fire until he blew the whistle, and this he did as soon as he could see the gray mass of figures advancing across No Man's Land in the weird light of a misty moon. The Germans received a very warm welcome from our particular part of the "Contemptible Little Army," and must have also had a rude awakening when we opened up with rapid fire with our Lee-Enfield rifles. They evidently thought the French were in front of them, until they heard our fire, but as they heard the rapid fire of the Lee-Enfields on previous occasions, it didn't take them long to know that the hated British were on the spot. "The Britishers' Mad Minute," was the name the Germans gave our rapid fire when they first experienced it at Mons, because they were astonished that infantry could average thirty rounds a minute per man. This speed could not be equaled by any other army at the time, the French being equipped with the Lebel rifle, which did not have a clip loading action, and the Germans, who relied more on their machine gun fire to break up infantry attacks, were amateurs in comparison to our army, where rifles were concerned.

The Germans were mowed down before they reached us, and although they made two further attacks during the night, we had not the opportunity to use the bayonet, the Germans being all killed or wounded before reaching our trench or ditch. The Germans gave up the attempt for the Messines Ridge and during the terrible winter campaign of 1914 and 1915 we did trench duty, three days in the front line and then three days in the reserve.

This awful monotonous life under the worst climatic conditions and living in a sea of mud was only brightened by one incident during the rest of the winter. The Germans hung up Chinese lanterns on Christmas Eve and sang carols, and both sides refrained from firing. During Christmas Day some of the bolder spirits of the German regiment opposite stood up on the parapet, and as none of our men would fire on them, an unofficial armistice was therefore on. Our men did likewise, and not a shot was fired, both sides believing in the old saying, "Peace and good will to all men on Christmas Day." This was the only time throughout the war that such an incident happened, as we received strict instructions not to fraternize with the enemy on account of their despicable and treacherous acts in bringing machine guns up under cover of stretcher bearers on several occasions when armistices were allowed to bury the dead shortly before Christmas.

When spring arrived, we were on tiptoe with excitement for the coming offensive, as we were fed up with the trenches and mud and wanted to get the Germans in the open.

The first offensive of the year 1915 was made by the British at Neuve Chapelle on March 10th, and several divisions, including our own, were massed in the vicinity a few days beforehand. Batteries of artillery to the number of five hundred guns were masked and hidden until they opened up for the preliminary bombardment. The Germans had no inkling of the coming attack, and the surprise it caused was a nasty knock to their boasted secret service and civilian spies, who were placed throughout Flanders years before the war, and who posed as Belgian and French farmers. They devised many schemes for informing the enemy what was happening, and on previous occasions they had been able to supply the Germans with accurate information by their windmill and other tricks. This time they were fooled, and when the bombardment commenced at 6.30 A.M. the Germans were at breakfast, according to the statements which the prisoners made when they were captured.

We had taken our positions in the front line trenches the night before and had erected trench climbing ladders for jumping over the parapets.

At 7 A.M. we went "Over the Top" in the first offensive our army made since trench warfare first began after the battle of the Aisne the previous October. At this time I was acting as company stretcher bearer, and therefore had to follow the company as they advanced across No Man's Land.

Although we had a large number of guns, we were very deficient in heavy artillery and howitzers, the majority being 18 pounder field guns and which proved a failure as a means to blast away the barbed wire and parapets of the German trenches and redoubts.

On part of the line where we attacked, the barbed wire was not destroyed and consequently we were held up and suffered terrible losses from machine gun fire. At last, some of our men broke through the wire by breaching it with wire clippers and then jumping in the trenches bayoneted German after German, from traverse to traverse until they were all accounted for in that part of the line.

Our losses were appalling during the few minutes it took to cut the wire, our casualties totaling over 750 men out of the thousand engaged. A young subaltern was the only officer who got through the engagement, the colonel, major, adjutant, and company commanders all being killed while leading the attack.

Our officers had all been in the army for a number of years and were excellent soldiers. We could ill afford to lose such men, as there were none who could fill their places, and we noticed a remarkable difference when the reinforcements arrived, the new officers being hastily trained and the ink stains not yet off their fingers.

The remnants of the battalion reached the German third line of trenches and there waited for reinforcements. For two days I carried the stretcher without a rest until at last I collapsed under the strain and had to rest for a few hours. How many men I carried I do not know, and the last few hours seemed like a dream, broken with the cries of the wounded.

My clothes were saturated with the blood of the men I bandaged and carried, and when I was finally relieved, I had to get a new suit from the quartermaster stores.

On the first night of the offensive, the Germans made a counter attack in a vain endeavor to recapture the redoubt, and the line of trenches called Port Arthur. During the attack, I was in the front line attending to wounded men who needed attention, and so I had a good view of the Germans as they were advancing.

They advanced, as was their custom, in close order, or mass formation. Our reinforcements, who had come up just after dark, had brought several machine guns, so we were quite prepared to give the Germans a fight to a finish. Our officers, knowing that the Germans could not break through our wire under the terrific hail of lead we would send over, gave strict orders not to fire until the Germans were up to the entanglements. Thus, at that short range, the slaughter would be much greater, and fewer Germans would reach back to their own lines during their consequent retreat.

There was not enough room on the parquet or firing platform for all our men, and the unlucky ones who were left standing at the bottom of the trench dragged some of the men on the parquets, so that they could get a few rounds off, and so settle "old scores" with "Fritz." Under the rapid fire of our machine guns and rifles the Germans were mowed down almost to a man, very few of even their swiftest runners making a home run.

I was in the trenches at Neuve Chapelle for a few more days until the remnants of our battalion were taken to the rear to be re-formed when the drafts arrived. After six days' rest we were again on trench duty, and this continued until May 9th, when our division was moved to Fromelles to participate in the offensive on that sector.

During the first part of this offensive our battalion acted as supports to the London Rifles, whose objective was the

German third line of trenches. When this objective was reached we received the order to advance in open formation. German machine guns opened up fire on us as we advanced, and men were soon dropping like flies.

My chum, who was carrying the other end of the stretcher, was riddled with machine gun bullets. It so happened that he was caught by the group shots from one gun. It was lucky for me that the German machine gunner was grouping his shots, and not using the traverse system, or I would have been hit also.

I was then left to carry the stretcher alone, and while advancing further saw our new colonel fall wounded, so I rushed to his assistance. The bone of his leg was smashed by a bullet, and as I went up to him he ordered me away, and told me to take cover or I would be killed, as the bullets by this time were flying around in hundreds. I walked a few paces and returned for another attempt to bandage him, but he again ordered me to take cover, so I said to him, "Well, if you don't want help, there are plenty around who do." This officer was Colonel Vandeleur, who was captured during the retreat of Mons, while in command of the Cheshire Regiment.

He escaped from the German prison camp, owing to the fact that he could speak the German language like a native, and when he reached London by way of Holland, he was granted an audience with the King, as he was the first Britisher to escape from Germany. After having a rest, he was again sent to France, and took command of our battalion.

Having lost my chum, I had to work single-handed, and this meant carrying wounded on my back. We remained at

Fromelles for three days and were under bombardment all the time, the Germans being heavily supplied with "Heavies" and a plentiful supply of "Jack Johnsons" and "Coal Boxes."

Our attack at Fromelles was not as successful as we had anticipated, owing to insufficient artillery support, and we were at a disadvantage during the year 1915 on account of the shortage in heavy artillery. The Germans, who had prepared for so many years beforehand, were plentifully supplied with all kinds of artillery from 77 MM. to 17-inch Skoda howitzers and for every shell we fired they fired ten.

Shortly after the Fromelles affair, I was wounded while in the front line, and remained in the hospital for three months. When I returned to the battalion, they were doing trench duty at Fleurbaix, and with only two minor engagements I suffered the agonies of trench warfare once more, this time for several months, including the winter of 1915 and 1916.

On the first of July, 1916, an offensive on the Somme was started and our division was now in the thick of it. This was a change from the previous engagements, as our munition and armament factories in Britain had been working at top pressure for months and we had ample supplies of guns and ammunition and could give "Fritz" shell for shell.

I had left the stretcher bearers and during the Somme offensive I was fighting in the ranks and went "Over the Top," this time with rifle and bayonet. After severe fighting, we took Friecourt, our first objective, and after entering the village the prisoners were collected, and I was detailed to escort prisoners to the cages, and to remain as one of the sentries until relieved. One of the prisoners who could speak English asked me if the men of our regiment were sailors, because at this time we wore the Scotch Balmoral Blach hats, and he evidently mistook them for sailors' hats, as they are not unlike the headgear of the British Navy, and it must have been the first time he had seen them, as most of the Scottish troops were the Glengarrys.

I quickly informed him that we were the famous Scottish Rifles, the old 90th of Foot who had made a reputation in previous wars, and who intended to keep up the reputation made by knocking Hell out of the Germans on every possible occasion. He was different than the rest of the prisoners, the majority of them being morose and sullen, so I kept up a conversation with him, and it was interesting at the time to listen to a German prisoner who could speak English, and who wished to tell me of the things that had happened to him. He had been a steward on one of the Hamburg-American Line boats plying between Germany and New York, and he had learned to speak English by talking to passengers. He said that he was glad to be captured, and for this information I handed him a few cigarettes.

Shortly after, I was again sent back to the front line, and during the next two weeks we advanced twenty miles, capturing Combles and other towns.

The battle of the Somme was the biggest offensive during 1916. Considerable ground was retaken, and thousands of Germans captured. We were sent to the Bethune front, which was at the time a quiet sector in comparison to the Somme, and there we did trench duty for six weeks before being returned once again to the Somme.

On the 23rd of October we again attacked and gained more ground. By this time the Somme battlefield was a land of shell-holes and mud. The hardships we had to undergo were terrible. The bombardments never ceased, and sometimes it increased to drum fire. For the next few months we remained on this front, this being my third winter in the trenches, I was beginning to be "fed up" with the whole thing.

I had had one seven days' leave to England at the end of 1915, and in November, 1916, I was granted one month's furlough on account of having completed my term as a time serving man.

The Conscription Act coming into force kept me on for the duration of the war, but in consideration of my long service, having completed my thirteenth year, as stipulated on my attestation, this special leave was granted. What a relief it was to know that for the next four weeks I would not hear the shells or stumble along in the mud up to my knees, and, sometimes, up to the waist.

How my mouth watered when I realized that I would get a change of diet from the everlasting bully beef and biscuits, commonly known as "hard tack." How pleasant to know that the "cooties" would soon be off me and a new change of clothing on my back. One can only appreciate good food and clean clothes after months of horror experienced by eating bully and biscuits and being tormented by "cooties," or, as we called them, "Wee Scunners."

During the month's furlough I spent in London, I had the time of my life, but as all good days have to end at some time or other, I was soon back in the trenches, and to make things worse, we were on the Somme.

Christmas day I again spent in the trenches, but this time there was no fraternizing, both sides being very bitter and for any of us to show a head above the parapet meant death from a German sniper.

We could never forget the Zeppelin raids, the sinking of the *Lusitania*, and the despicable treachery of the enemy on every occasion, wherever they got a chance. The Germans proved themselves worse than the lowest savages, and Lord Kitchener said that they were worse than the Dervishes of the Soudan, the fanatics of the desert. Never will a British soldier forget the incident where British soldiers were burned alive, by the orders of Prince Rupprecht of Bavaria, and the crucifying of the Canadians at Ypres.

In the spring of 1917 the Germans retreated to a new line of defense, and for three weeks we advanced under cover of the night, throwing out patrols, to try and get in touch with the Germans. This was a welcome change, as there was no firing, and as we were on the move it was less monotonous than being in the trenches. The Germans had destroyed everything in their retreat, farm houses being blown up, orchards cut down, cross roads destroyed, and every trick, the Germans who are past masters in this kind of thing, knew so well how to do. The countryside was laid waste, and I saw hundreds of dead men who had been left behind by the Germans, unburied, and left to rot; most of them had been mangled by shell-fire and it was sights such as these that make men think of the terrible folly of war, and why such things should be.

We have one consolation, and that is, the men of the Allies who were killed did not die in vain, as the objects for which we entered the war have been achieved and the wrongs will be righted.

At last we got in touch with the Germans and dug ourselves in, and then we had another spell of trench duty, until taken away from the Somme and moved up to Belgium to participate in the Paschendale offensive in June, 1917. Of all the fronts I was ever on, Paschendale was the worst. The front included the Ypres salient where fighting had been going on almost incessantly from October, 1914. Neither side made much progress, and during these three years the ground had changed hands many times and was mostly shell-holes. In fact, for miles it was difficult to find a few square yards untouched by shells, and I think that more men were killed in the Ypres salient than any other place of its size in the world. It was impossible to build trenches on this front, and the system of defense was to fortify shell-holes with sand bags, two or three men to a shell-hole. I was in one advance which we made under cover of the biggest barrage thrown over at that time, and when our objective was reached, we manned the shell-holes until relieved.

In September, 1917, I was sent to a bombing school, and went through a course which I passed, and was then qualified to act as a bombing instructor when I arrived back to the battalion. The course lasted one month, and in that time I learned all there was to know about bombs, especially the deadly Mills bomb, with its three and a half to five seconds time fuse. I found bombing more interesting than any other kind of warfare I had yet taken up, and the fact that it was possible to kill or wound a number of Germans with one well-aimed bomb greatly appealed to me. When I returned to the line my rifle was placed as second favorite, the bombs always holding first place in my estimation.

When I arrived back to the battalion, they were at Ploegsteert, or "Plug-street," as we called it, and this front being rather quick, we had a picnic, in comparison to some of the previous places. The trenches at Ploegsteert were well constructed, and fairly dry, and were always considered the best on the British front.

The Germans were 1,300 yards away and a small river ran between their lines and ours. Owing to the great distance between the lines, patrols were always out at night, so as to prevent a surprise attack. Our patrols consisted of a non-commissioned officer and two men, but sometimes a fighting patrol of ten men with a Lewis gun were sent out.

As the Germans always had patrols out as well, this was a ticklish business, as it was quite common for the patrols to meet and then there would be a little dirty work. On these occasions I always had a good supply of bombs, and one night when near a bridge of planks, which crossed the river, I heard the creaking and knew that a German patrol was crossing. The night being pitch dark, made it impossible for me to see them, so I whispered to the two privates to creep back to the bushes, which were a few yards away, and there we would wait for them. This we did in a few seconds. I could hear the German patrol walking through the grass toward us, and when I judged they were about twenty-five yards away I quickly removed the safety pin from the bomb and threw it in their direction.

By the time the first one burst, I had the pin removed from another one, and as the place was lit up by the flash of the bomb, I had a good view of the German fighting patrol, and so consequently the second bomb which I threw fell in the middle of them, as they were beating it for the bridge, and evidently some of them were hit, as they squealed like most Germans do when wounded. Knowing that the survivors would open fire in our direction as soon as they were over the bridge, we ran for cover to a bunch of trees, and there lay down for a few minutes until the firing had died down.

Telling my two chums to remain under cover until I returned, I crawled back to see if the Germans had returned for any of their wounded. Carefully maneuvering, I could hear the low moans of a wounded German, so I went to see what damage I had done. One German was dead and the other who was moaning was severely wounded in the legs, several pieces of the bomb hitting him in different places.

Seeing that he needed immediate assistance, and wishing to get him back to our lines for information purposes, I crawled back to my chums and told them to come back with me to the wounded German. When we reached him I told one of them to go down to the bridge and watch in case the Germans would return. The first thing I did was to kick the German's rifle out of the way, in case he wanted to use it when our backs were turned, and then proceeded to bandage his wounds. Then walking down to the bridge, I told my chum that everything was ready to carry the prisoner back, and after stumbling and carrying him for over a thousand yards, we reached our lines, and then handed him over to the stretcher bearers, who took him to the dressing station.

After a few weeks at Ploegsteert, we were again shifted to Passchendale, and as the winter was now on, things were much worse than on our previous visit. The first time we went to the front line we experienced on this occasion something new. Previously, in the trenches, we always had ration parties go back to the rear at night for supplies, and always received rations daily and a lot of rum in the morning.

The shell-fire being so bad made it too costly at Passchendale to send men back every night, so before we went up the line, we were served with three days' rations and a gasoline can full of water. In addition to this, every man had to carry 250 rounds of ammunition, several bombs, gas mask, trench coat and waterproof sheet, rifle, bayonet and grubber, sand bags, trench helmet, and a shovel. I shall never forget the six miles' march up to the front line with all the equipment. The shovel which I had tied to the middle of my back kept banging against my legs, and I was always scared of losing my can of water. Several men, while crossing the duck-boards fell off, and went up to their necks in mud, and if curses would have killed the Kaiser, he would have died that night.

At last we reached the front line and relieved the Devons, who had been up there three days—three days in a shell-hole, half full of water, bully beef, biscuits, and cold water, tainted with gasoline for our rations, shell-fire continuously and occasionally a cloud of gas.

I do not think it possible for a person who has never experienced it to have the slightest imagination what suffering and torture we had to undergo on the Passchendale front. Many a wounded man, while staggering back over the duck-board, slipped off and was drowned, not having the strength to pull himself out of the mud.

Fatigue parties were working every night to keep the

duck-board paths in repair, as shells were continuously hitting them, and every hit meant a few duck-boards smashed to splinters. The dump where new supplies of duck-boards were kept was five miles from the front line, and if new ones were required it meant a five-mile hike with a duck-board on our shoulders, and a five-mile hike back. We lost thirty men out of a fatigue party one night by shell-fire, and the casualties were so heavy that there was a continuous stream of motor ambulances along the roads in the rear.

This was my fourth winter in the trenches, and the constant strain was beginning to tell on me, and I fell sick with pneumonia and developed trench feet. This time I was sent to England, and when I came out of the hospital I obtained convalescent leave to see my people, who were living in Winnipeg, Canada.

My health not improving, I was discharged from the army in May, 1918, after having served fifteen years as a regular soldier and was three years and two months in France.